Bring No Clothes
Bloomsbury and the Philosophy of Fashion

Charlie Porter

PENGUIN BOOKS

PENGUIN BOOKS

UK | USA | Canada | Ireland | Australia
India | New Zealand | South Africa

Penguin Books is part of the Penguin Random House group of companies whose addresses can be found at global.penguinrandomhouse.com.

First published in Particular Books 2023
Published with a new Afterword in Penguin Books 2024
002

Typeset by Jouve (UK), Milton Keynes
Printed in Germany by GGP Media GmbH, Poessneck

A CIP catalogue record for this book is available from the British Library

ISBN: 978-1-802-06114-7

www.greenpenguin.co.uk

PENGUIN BOOKS

Bring No Clothes

'Charlie Porter is a magician, a radical historian who has pulled away all the threadbare myths about Bloomsbury, using clothes as a way of revealing the vulnerable bodies and wild new ideas of Woolf and her circle. *Bring No Clothes* is at once an enriching account of the past and a primer for the future: a guide to how we too can clothe our bodies for freedom' Olivia Laing

'Excellent . . . Porter's generous, empathetic eye feels like a corrective for the more salacious historical depictions of the Bloomsbury Group's affairs . . . *Bring No Clothes* doesn't just introduce a new frame of thinking, it adds a fresh layer of humanity to the collective' Patrick Sproull, *Independent*

'Charlie Porter applies a literary critic's close reading to the clothes of the early twentieth century, unpicking philosophical texts from their textures. *Bring No Clothes* offers a way of recalibrating the world by understanding the tensions that underpin and overdetermine it through the ways we dress. With curiosity and contemporaneity, he finds in the Bloomsbury Group's experiments in intimacy a queer possibility for the way we live today' Sam Buchan-Watts, author of *Path Through Wood*

'Spot-on . . . the way the [Bloomsbury] circle thought about clothes was part of a wider revolt . . . Thanks to his access to the contents of several Bloomsbury wardrobes, together with a trove of previously unseen photographs, Porter is able to provide a detailed illustration of how "Make it new" played out on the material level' Kathryn Hughes, *Guardian*

'One of the best books about Bloomsbury!' Maggie Humm, author and Vice Chair of the Virginia Woolf Society

'Fascinating' Samira Ahmed, *BBC Front Row*

'Unlocks the Bloomsbury Group's wardrobes to expose the intricate interplay between attire, liberation and control' *Vogue*

'A deep dive into the wardrobes of the Bloomsbury Group. Behind colour choices and hemlines are fascinating insights into their bodies and minds' *Monocle*

'Porter clearly enjoys [the Bloomsbury Group's] company – exploring how Virginia Woolf's loose, long-line garments, John Maynard Keynes's "soft tailoring", Vanessa Bell's wildly colourful home-made dresses, photographs of a naked Duncan Grant, and the loosening of E. M. Forster's buttoned-up suits all demonstrate the radicalism of a group of people determined to live differently' Anna Leszkiewicz, *New Statesman*

'Fresh, empathetic . . . personal as much as intellectual . . . *Bring No Clothes* might be read as the manifesto of a queer human' Sophie Oliver, *Times Literary Supplement*

'A radical account, unbuttoning the artistic and sexual mavericks that were the Bloomsbury Group . . . he's come up with some answers as to why we wear what we wear now . . . Porter has beautifully crafted his text into an eclectic mix of six personal deep dives, following some of Britain's most influential figures in literature and art . . . a revelatory telling of a moment in history . . . he's managed to uncover unanswered questions and create a manifesto for dressing today, meaning it's a must-read for fashion anarchists, admirers and anyone in between' *10magazine*

'An elegant and thoughtful investigation into the psychological space that clothes took up in the heads of the Bloomsbury Group . . . Porter reminds us how what we wear is a clear marker of social position and a means by which one can pass through life through visual codes . . . Porter deftly shows the reader how and why clothes matter at all levels of their use: however beautiful or workaday, fashion tells us much about who the Bloomsbury Group were, about who Porter is – and something of who we are, too' India Lewis, *The Arts Desk*

ABOUT THE AUTHOR

Charlie Porter is a writer, fashion critic and curator. He has written for *The Financial Times*, the *Guardian*, *The New York Times*, *GQ*, *Luncheon*, *i-D* and *Fantastic Man*, and has been described as one of the most influential fashion journalists of his time. Porter co-runs the London queer rave Chapter 10, and is a trustee of the Friends of Arnold Circus, where he is also a volunteer gardener. He lives in London.

Contents

Introduction 1

Virginia Woolf 19

The Dreadnought Hoax and the visual language of power 56

Vanessa Bell 65

Measuring Wardrobes, or, Where did they put all their stuff? 102

Duncan Grant 113

The Apostles, and conversations about style 140

E. M. Forster 149

Two Stracheys and Carrington, or, The veil of clothing 196

John Maynard Keynes 207

What the Bloomsbury servants wore 252

Lady Ottoline Morrell 263

Bloomsbury, fashion, philosophy 314

Postscript 334

And then . . . 340

Special Thanks and Acknowledgements 345

Quotation Reference Sources 348

List of Photographic Credits 357

Bring No Clothes

On a Wednesday in September, Virginia Woolf wrote to T. S. Eliot. It was 1920, five years before the publication of *Mrs Dalloway*, two years before *The Waste Land*. She was 38, he was about to turn 32.

'We are hoping to see you on Saturday,' Woolf wrote from Monk's House, her home in the remote village of Rodmell, East Sussex. The letter is short. She gives instructions about the best train to take: the 11.55, or the 3.20. She says they would send 'a trap' – a horse-drawn carriage. The letter concludes: 'Please bring no clothes: we live in a state of the greatest simplicity.'

Woolf had used such words before. Ten years earlier, in December 1910, she wrote to her first love, Violet Dickinson. 'My Violet, I will come on Saturday with great pleasure – no clothes – not very clean.'

A year later, she sent a postcard to her soon-to-be husband, Leonard Woolf. He was about to make his first visit to Firle in East Sussex, where she was renting a house: 'Please bring no clothes.'

Her sister, Vanessa Bell, was already using similar language. On the third of November 1909, she wrote to her future comrade, the artist and key Bloomsbury figure Duncan Grant. Bell invited Grant to dine the following Tuesday, stating: 'don't trouble to dress'.

These few words encapsulate a seismic societal shift.

By 'clothes', Woolf meant the traditional fashions of her Victorian upbringing. This was an oppressive world codified by garments, with outfit changes throughout the day, leading to the nightly crescendo of dressing for dinner.

It sounds so innocuous. What's wrong with dressing for dinner?

The rigid, inhibitive clothing worn by women for centuries – cinched, trussed, prettified – manifested the control of a patriarchal society. It was a society that cast women as mere fodder for marriage. For centuries, women were expected to wear restrictive clothes, the garments themselves often the products of oppression: of the colonialization, enslavement and exploitation that lay behind the global cotton industry.

'Dressing for dinner' cemented hierarchies of class, power and gender. Whenever we 'dress for dinner' today, we continue to perpetuate these hierarchies. It is in each of our power to change this, through simple but affirmative acts.

All Woolf needed to say was 'bring no clothes'. Her meaning: come as you are. We are no longer living by those rules. We refuse them, we reject them, we are pushing for something new. If we were to accept Woolf's invitation, we could 'bring no clothes' to our own lives, breaking from preconceptions to forge new ways of being.

The Bloomsbury group was a loose collective of artists, writers and thinkers, first formed in London at the beginning of the 20th century. As their friendships and alliances grew, they opened up to the possibilities of sexual, creative and intellectual exploration. They evolved relationships and environments within which queer desire could be expressed and nourished. The core collective of siblings, friends and lovers would talk without inhibition about sex, philosophy, art, literature, politics.

At its centre were the Stephen sisters, Virginia and Vanessa, twentysomethings who had just freed themselves from their stifling family: no more would they suffer its abuses in silence. They created a space where, for the first time, they could live beyond expectation.

Bloomsbury members would go on to have profound impact on global culture: literature, art, economics and politics. Together, they explored modes of living that liberated sexuality. They embraced feminism, queerness and pacificism. They believed in creativity as a way of being. They pushed against the gender binary. Their cross-disciplinary, multi-layered existence was unique: a group that showed signs of gender parity in the still male-dominated arenas of art, literature and politics.

These changes amounted to a fresh philosophy of living. This involved a new way with clothes. For the women especially, their loose and long garments, often hand-crafted or repaired, were an emancipation from the constraints and formality of the past. This was a manifestation of their radicalism, a lived experience of philosophy for those denied a full university education due to gender, and therefore denied its dialogue, intellectual community, betterment.

Retrospectively, their style has become known as the 'Bloomsbury Look', a pioneering romanticism and decorativeness that has inspired 21st-century catwalk shows from brands and designers such as Comme des Garçons, Dior, Fendi, Burberry, Erdem and S.S. Daley. Often, it's not just the group's look that is emulated, but their ideas that have sparked new fashion design.

But we can do more with their clothing than use it just for style inspiration. By taking what they wore as primary evidence, untold narratives and hidden lives emerge. We can tell a different story of Bloomsbury, one that cuts away the myths and gossip, letting its characters reveal more of themselves, whether we like what is revealed, or otherwise. At the same time, we can gain fresh insights into the historical origins of the clothing that we wear today. This can then help us rethink our own approach to dressing.

For centuries, society had been bound by strict modes of dress. Ballgowns, petticoats, crinolines, corsets: TV shows and period films can make us believe such a life was glorious, full of intrigue, blushed cheeks and stolen glances. Maybe for the privileged few it was.

In reality, most people were kept in their place by clearly demarcated differences in dress. The wealth and status of the empowered and moneyed were displayed by the extremity of the silhouette, the quality of the fabric, the complexity of the handiwork and the cleanness of the garments themselves.

The cinched and petticoated garments made for women were an easy way of keeping them in a state of discomfort and subservience. Men were stuffed into frock coats and supposed finery, their peacockery geared to maintaining a patriarchal status quo, with silhouette and embellishment evolved from military dress, evoking power and prowess. Queer humans had little choice but to conform.

The working and middle classes were meant to be in thrall to the fancy clothing of the upper classes. It's not that different today: in fashion museums and stately homes, we pay money to look reverently at the sanctified garments of the privileged. Would we do the same to look at historical workers' clothes? We can't know, because barely any exist. In previous centuries, workers' garments were worn until they could be worn no more. Any remaining fabric would be used for cloths, patchwork, or whatever purpose it could serve.

As the Bloomsbury group formed, rigid societal structure was beginning to break down, due to accelerating urbanization, technological advances and the efforts of those fighting for social and political change. It was a crucial breakpoint. Women would claim more freedom in dressing. Men would be released from frock coats and tails. Queer people would find more routes to self-expression through clothing.

Meanwhile the garments of working classes would become more durable, more enjoyable to wear. Eventually these garments, like jeans, would become the choice of middle and upper classes. In the shifts of the early 20th century are the roots of how we all dress today.

The Bloomsbury group was formed of humans engaged in radical change, at a moment of radical historical change. I know of no other collective like theirs at that time, so open to progressive thinking, gender equality and queerness. By using some of its key members as case studies, we can gain insight into the connections between sartorial and social change; how change happened or was resisted, how we might change ourselves, and how we might break through any resistance to change.

This is not to say that we can hold up the Bloomsbury group as model citizens. Its members were upper and upper middle class; most relied on servants, whose lives were often miserable. 'I do not wonder that people commit suicide, or even murder,' wrote Bell's new housekeeper, Grace Germany, later Grace Higgens, on 29 April 1922. She was 18 years old. 'Life sometimes grows so monotonous, there is no wish to live.'

Members of the group frequently used racist and anti-Semitic language. In 1910, Woolf and Duncan Grant were among six who wore blackface and costumes, pretending to be members of the Abyssinian royal family in what became known as the Dreadnought Hoax.

To study the Bloomsbury group does not mean wanting to be the Bloomsbury group. They had certain freedoms because of their immense privilege, and were able to exercise those freedoms within the safety of their walls, or the privacy of their land. Their liberation happened within a society that continued to rely on colonialism and land control for its affluence, with the British Empire staking claim to a quarter of the planet's land area in the 1920s.

This does not make the Bloomsbury group unworthy of study. In fact, it makes it more crucial. If we can unlock the oppressive power structures of a century ago, we can begin to unlock those that still exist today.

By focusing on their clothes, we can approach the Bloomsbury group from a fresh angle. Rather than seeing their story as a tight weave, rigid and unwieldy, we can join them in the laying down of their threads, letting in air to their many moments of possibility and change.

Imagine we're in a space-station science lab. We will observe six members of the Bloomsbury group as if they are on petri dishes: Virginia Woolf, Vanessa Bell, Duncan Grant, E. M. Forster, John Maynard Keynes and Lady Ottoline Morrell. Each was early-era Bloomsbury: young adults by the turn of the 20th century, active during the switch from Victorian to modern, rather than those born later who benefited from this change. The six have been specifically chosen to explore different facets of clothing and society, then and now: gender and sexuality, patriarchy, power, repression, self-realization, personal autonomy.

Throughout, clothing will help us look again at well-trodden narratives, so many of which are short sighted or just plain wrong. Virginia Woolf, for example, has been gaslighted and labelled 'mad'; her marriage treated like a bond of tradition rather than a positive strategy for living a non-conforming life; her queerness seen as a curious amusement.

Virginia Woolf was queer. She found physical pleasure and sexual fulfilment with women, most notably with Vita Sackville-West, yet she did not define herself as a 'Sapphist' – the term she used for lesbian.

Men did not interest her, yet at that time, seemingly heterosexual marriage was a common solution for queer humans. Before she accepted the proposal of her husband, Leonard Woolf, she wrote to him to say, 'As I told you brutally the other day, I feel no physical attraction in you. There are moments – when you kissed me the other day was one – when I feel no more than a rock.'

With the letter, she included a photograph. Woolf is hooded, in knits. It's a visual manifestation of her feeling no more than a rock.

If Woolf were alive today, we might imagine her identifying as non-binary or trans, particularly from reading her novel *Orlando: A Biography*, whose lead character transitions from male to female. Woolf appeared alien to her own gendered physicality.

It is uncontroversial to call Woolf queer. It allows us to openly describe the life she lived and which, because of the repression of the time, she was prevented from living fully. I describe myself as 'queer' rather than 'gay', even though I am a gay male. I prefer it. The word is specific enough to have meaning, broad enough to give all queer humans the space to be themselves.

It is important to call Woolf queer, because for nearly a century, Woolf biographers have tiptoed round the subject, talking of her love for Sackville-West and Dickinson as jolly japes, pivoting her life instead around men. Recognizing her queerness is crucial to understanding her work, just as queerness is crucial to understanding the lives and work of Carrington and Lady Ottoline Morrell, other married Bloomsbury women whose stories break heteronormal narratives.

This honesty about queerness is non-salacious, non-prurient. To be honest about queerness is to be honest about human life. The queer members of the Bloomsbury group had to navigate prohibitive societal norms to find ways to exist. By looking at their clothing, these strategies for living come to the fore. It can make us realize that, even today, we all live by such codes, as much as we believe that we are free.

The act of getting dressed is an act of thinking through clothes. Even at its most mundane, dressing is thinking. 'I am cold. I need a sweater': that is thinking, in response to bodily needs. 'I like this sweater, I'll wear it': that is thinking, activated by personal taste and pleasure. If a kid wears something wild because, 'I hate my parents, I want to upset them': that is thinking, making use of clothing's blunt emotional force.

We can even claim to dress unthinkingly: 'I wear this suit to work every day. I put it on without thinking.' But this is still thinking, tuned into the historic layers of meaning that have made tailoring the garment of authority and power.

We usually don't prioritize this thinking. There are likely more pressing issues: how am I going to pay the bills this month, can I afford my rent, how are the people I love, what's the news, how crushed do I feel by global events, how powerless.

Because we don't prioritize this thinking through clothing, we consider it insignificant. Yet the clothes we put on each morning can lock us in acquiescence to the structures of power that we find so crushing. If we were to pay more attention to our thinking through clothing, we could begin to wriggle loose.

This is a simple meaning of the philosophy of fashion.

It is accessible to all of us, once we overcome any embarrassment we may feel about taking ourselves seriously. We are all experts in the language of clothing. We all understand the power of a uniform, the authority of tailoring, the veneer of togetherness represented by neat clothes, the supposed shambles of the messy.

And yet, most of us deny our expertise. Ask someone in fashion about how they dress and they'll likely put themselves down, say they just throw things on – 'What, this thing?' – or brush it off like you're an annoyance for asking. Meanwhile, those outside of fashion can feel like they are clueless, as if there are secrets about style just beyond their grasp that are being withheld from them, or that fashion is so remote to them as to be meaningless. All these stances ignore the simple fact that we all already understand the messages and meaning in clothes.

The Bloomsbury group came into adulthood at an epochal moment, when this expertise in clothing helped many of them to alter their very mode of living. They could think through their clothing, and make change through their clothing.

It was not true of all. Bloomsbury members that did not make change through their clothing will also provide us with fresh fields of study.

I have a degree in Philosophy. At school, I wanted to be a writer, but didn't know what to study at university. I was young in my year, not turning 18 till months after I sat my A-levels: English, History, Russian. I took a gap year and chose a university course during my break. I'd never studied Philosophy before. It sounded fun. I applied.

It was 1992. King's College London gave me a place. The three-year course put little obligation on its students. One hour a week was registered. Most of my time went to student journalism, and then, in my final year, work experience at *Vogue*. After I sat my finals, I went straight to an internship at *GQ*.

For years, I thought little more of philosophy. Yet recently, my studies, previously dormant, have resonated again in the way I write about fashion, art, life.

Ludwig Wittgenstein studied at King's College, Cambridge a few years after the early Bloomsbury group members, and knew some of them as friends. He was queer, living a spartan life. His writing is mostly impenetrable, cut with sudden moments of extreme clarity.

Much of his thinking is simplified into the saying 'only describe, don't explain', though what he actually wrote was, 'We must do away with all explanation, and description alone must take its place.'

Fashion writing can get stuck trying to explain, usually trends or styles, often creating a remove from the reader. This book will attempt a different path. It is a chance for me to describe, to do philosophy through fashion.

For this, I will Orlando myself. We need to break any gendered assumptions about garments, so we can consider these humans as individuals in their clothes and their circumstances.

In the end, this is a book about love. It is about the roots of what the writer bell hooks called 'the lovelessness that is so pervasive in our society'. Really, what we are studying through these characters and their clothes is their experiences of love, of love denied, love outlawed, love repressed, or lovelessness.

The Bloomsbury group attempted to experience love in full-hearted ways, whether it be love with their sexual partners, their friends, or love at the centre of their politics, particularly their commitment to pacifism. They were often thwarted, usually by societal norms or laws that prevented their love.

We all use clothing to attract, flirt, or to repel. We take off our clothing to make love. We can use our clothing to express – or to conceal – our queerness. The clothes of Woolf, Carrington and Morrell help us to shine light on the experiences of queer women in the early 20th century – their experiences mostly overlooked. But garments can also be used to mask queerness, as we'll find in the tailoring of John Maynard Keynes as well as E. M. Forster, who would write about the 'undeveloped hearts' of men in his essay 'Notes on the English Character'. We will discover the role of garments in the denial of love in a patriarchal, heteronormative society.

I want to write with love. I have often found journalism to cast a veil over how I truly felt. I have written truthfully, have tried to get to the heart of what I wanted to say, and could often get close to what I meant, but not go all the way. I now want to write about love, and to connect clothing, and philosophy, to the possibility of love.

We will often deal with absences. Barely any garments worn by any of these humans still exist. There are no photographs of the early Bloomsbury gatherings, from 1904–1910. How come? Considering why there are no clothes, no photographs, will help us better understand them.

We will also challenge the language of clothing. Different members of the Bloomsbury group were described by their contemporaries as 'badly dressed'. Those words are so damning. But what do they mean? To me, being badly dressed is a positive. I am appallingly dressed. My new grey sweater already has four moth holes. I have no smart trousers/jacket/shoes. I don't go anywhere that would need me to wear smart trousers/jacket/shoes.

I have always been like this. Because I have worked in fashion for two decades, I have created a psychological space for myself in which I can dress in ways that interest me.

That last sentence: I originally wrote, 'in which I can dress however I want'. Then I realized it wasn't true. I am restricted by societal pressures as much as anyone. I am nearly 50. I want to break free.

While writing this book, I have also been researching an exhibition for Charleston, the former home of Vanessa Bell and Duncan Grant. Through this research, I have been given the most extraordinary access: rummaging through boxes of photographs in the attic, unpacking long-stored bits of cloth, spending time in the house outside of visiting hours, and meeting with descendants of Bloomsbury members.

There were big surprises for me in other institutions and public libraries, particularly the diaries of Charleston housekeeper Grace Higgens and the clothes of Lady Ottoline Morrell. There are also mistakes that need correcting.

In 1924, Woolf was photographed for *Vogue* by its chief photographers, Maurice Beck and Helen MacGregor. It has become commonly accepted that she did so wearing a dress of her mother's, Julia Stephen.

Her mother's dress! The psychological implications! Victorian, fussy, totally out of fashion at the time. What was she trying to say?

An image from the shoot first appeared in the Early May

1924 issue of *Vogue*. It was small on the page. Two years later, the image was given a page to itself, in the Early May issue.

Woolf, and that dress, in *Vogue*:

But wait. There are no photographs of her mother wearing this dress, or any dress cut in this way, revealing her lower neck, shoulder, upper chest. There are many photographs of Julia Stephen: her aunt was the photographer Julia Margaret Cameron. She wore dresses that covered her body. Here is Woolf's mother in a typical pose and garment, captured by Cameron.

Below is the most revealing her dresses get: a lace neck over the collarbone, then a keyhole opening to suggest decolletage, but the skin of her chest is covered over in black lace.

Nothing she wears in the photos I have studied has the flounce and ostentation of the dress in the *Vogue* portrait. Also, Woolf and her mother were around the same height, yet the dress looks oversized.

Woolf does not record the portraits being taken in her diaries. Surely, if she was making such a statement by wearing her mother's dress, she would have mentioned it. Indeed, when she returned to the same studio in 1925, she talks of the location as the place where a sculptor once worked, who had wanted to propose to her mother. No mention of the portrait that had been taken there involving her mother's dress.

There is no mention of it being her mother's dress in the biography written by her nephew, Quentin Bell, who was twelve when the portrait was taken. His ear was attuned to family lore and handed-down stories. This wasn't one of them. I can find no mention of it being her mother's dress anywhere.

There are no archives to check about Woolf photographs at Vogue House. All the prints of this pacifist, all records, were pulped in 1942, a year after her death, for raw materials in the war effort.

I emailed Maggie Humm, the writer and academic who is Vice-Chair of the Virginia Woolf Society. She agreed, and said that, in the opinion of the Society, it was not her mother's dress. We began referring to it as NHMD. Whose dress was it? I have my own theory, which we'll come to later.

This is how we will approach each of our subjects: what we think we know; what we actually know; what is in plain sight, waiting to be discovered, if we just let the clothes and their wearers speak.

Virginia Woolf

Virginia Woolf and Vanessa Bell were born at the end of a dead-end street. I'm standing outside it now – 22 Hyde Park Gate in South Kensington, London – at the bottom of a cul-de-sac, both grand and isolated.

The district had been fields not long before, then developed in the mid-19th century. An acquaintance of their father, Leslie Stephen, recalled visiting for tea, served in the basement. Virginia and her sister Vanessa sat there 'in plain black dresses with white lace collars and wrist bands'. At the tea, the sisters barely spoke.

It's likely their mother, Julia Stephen, was already dead. She died in 1895, aged 49. During her life, she had given birth to seven children. She would pass on a rigidity of deportment to Virginia.

Nearly 30 years later, in September 1924, the author Thomas Hardy was visited by the Bloomsbury patron Lady Ottoline Morrell. He asked her if she knew Woolf. Morrell told him that Woolf was 'very beautiful like a cameo'.

Cameos are engravings, often portraits, in stiff relief. In the 18th and 19th centuries, they had become popular in jewellery, such as brooches.

At the time, Hardy was 84, wearing a three-piece tweed suit, shirt and tie. His first editor had been Woolf's father, Leslie Stephen. Morrell recorded Hardy's response in her diary: '"That is just like her mother",' Hardy said, and he 'copied the way her mother entered a room – very stately like a cameo.'

Morrell took this photograph of Hardy on that visit where he impersonated Woolf's mother, stately like a cameo.

Here are Julia and Leslie Stephen, in 1893, sitting tight on a mean sofa, bodies covered in their Victorian clothes. The parents are acting like there's no one else in the room, but someone is operating the camera, and behind the sofa is Virginia, staring straight into the lens.

When she was a small child, Woolf was abused by their half-brother, Gerald Duckworth. Woolf detailed the abuse in *Sketch of the Past*, the memoir she left unfinished when she took her own life in 1941. The abuse caused her lifelong trauma triggered by her own image, especially when caught in a mirror. 'At any rate, the looking-glass shame has lasted all my life,' she wrote in 1939. 'Everything to do with dress – to be fitted, to come into a room wearing a new dress – still frightens me; at least makes me shy, self-conscious, uncomfortable.'

Here is Woolf with Duckworth in 1897, Woolf in restrictive Victorian dress, with a bound waist and completely covered body.

That year, Woolf had likely been made to wear stays, the common name for a corset, for the first time. She was not happy. On 1 April 1897, April Fool's Day, she wrote in her diary, 'I was forced to wear certain underclothing for the first time in my life.'

As a widower, their father was tyrannical, uncaring, resentful. For seven years, from the ages of 15 and 18 respectively, Virginia and Vanessa's lives were controlled by their other half-brother, George Duckworth, who sexually and psychologically abused them. Here is Woolf, in that stomach-bound silhouette, with her older half-sister, Stella, beside her, and George Duckworth smiling in the background.

Stella died in 1897, after which Duckworth's tyranny began. Part of his psychological abuse was his control of their clothing.

'I shrink from the years 1897–1904, the seven unhappy years,' Woolf wrote in *Sketch of the Past*. 1904 was the year her father died and the sisters escaped to Bloomsbury, the year Woolf turned 22, Bell 25. 'Not many lives were tortured and fretted and made numb with non-being as ours were then.'

Their days were locked into a stultifying Victorian cycle where men worked, women waited, then entertained. Mornings gave them brief freedom, any education taking place in the scant hours before their social responsibilities. 'I read and wrote. For three hours we lived in the world which we still inhabit,' wrote Woolf. 'For at this moment (November 1940) she [Vanessa] is painting at Charleston; and I am writing here in the garden room at Monks House. Nor would our clothes be very different; the skirts a little shorter perhaps. My hair not much tidier then than now; and Vanessa in a blue cotton smock; as no doubt she is at this moment.'

Each day, this false freedom was short-lived. 'Victorian society began to exert its pressure at about half past four,' wrote Woolf. For a young woman in Victorian England, this pressure was all about appearance, both to please society and to secure a husband. First, they had to be 'tidied and in our places' for tea. Then evening came.

'At seven thirty we went upstairs to dress,' she wrote. 'However cold or foggy, we slipped off our day clothes and stood shivering in front of wash basins. Each basin had its can of hot water. Neck and arms had to be scrubbed, for we had to enter the drawing room at eight with bare arms, low neck, in evening dress.'

Duckworth, who had his own income, expected a high standard of dress from his half-sisters, garments the Stephens could ill afford. Virginia once tried to cut costs, having an evening dress made from green furniture fabric.

'It was not velvet; nor plush; something betwixt and between; and for chairs, presumably, not dresses.'

Dressed, she presented herself to Duckworth, sitting in the drawing room in dinner jacket and black tie. 'He at once fixed on me that extraordinarily observant scrutiny with which he always inspected our clothes,' she wrote. 'He looked me up and down for a moment as if I were a horse brought into the show ring.'

He was not pleased. 'Then the sullen look came into his eyes; the look which expressed not simply aesthetic disapproval; but something that went deeper. It was the look of moral, of social, disapproval, as if he scented some kind of insurrection, of defiance of his accepted standards.'

The dress did not pass muster. 'He said at last: "Go and tear it up." He spoke in a curiously tart, rasping, peevish voice; the voice of the enraged male; the voice which expressed his serious displeasure at this infringement of a code that meant more to him than he could admit.'

At night, after forcing her to attend society parties, he would enter her bed.

Sexual, psychological. Duckworth subjected both Woolf and Bell to cruelty and control using clothes. In the summer of 1903, Woolf wrote to Violet Dickinson, her first true love. She was 21. 'Have you any stays?' she wrote. 'I tried to saw mine through this morning, but couldn't. What iron boned conventionality we live in . . .'

Woolf was due to visit Dickinson that Friday. She ended her letter by saying, 'I will lick you tenderly.' Woolf soon wrote to Dickinson saying, 'it is astonishing what depths – hot volcano depths – your finger has stirred . . .'

Violet with Virginia. The stirrer and the volcano. Queer magnetism shrouded.

Their dress very much followed the fashion of the era. The leading label in London was Lucile Ltd, the work of Lady Duff-Gordon, who started her fashion line in 1893. She is thought to have staged the first ever fashion show. Duff-Gordon often named her designs to convey emotion. This dress, of extreme cinched waist, was sketched for the autumn 1905 collection. It is called 'The tender grace of a day that is dead'.

Lucile Ltd was said to be the first global couture brand, with branches in Chicago, New York and Paris. In 1912, Duff-Gordon and her husband, Cosmo, used a pseudonym to board the RMS *Titanic*. Their cabin was A-16. On the night of 14 April, the Duff-Gordons and their secretary were among twelve passengers in a lifeboat that could have carried forty. Her husband later claimed the £5 he gave to the lifeboat's sailor-in-charge was not a bribe to not return and save those in the water.

In 1904, Virginia and Vanessa moved across the city to 46 Gordon Square, Bloomsbury, a London district just south of the three main railway stations for the north. 'Everything was going to be new,' Woolf wrote in 1920, 'everything was going to be different. Everything was on trial.'

This included their clothes. In 1905, their brother Thoby began bringing round his male friends from Cambridge. They would meet on Thursday evenings at Virginia and Vanessa's home. These weekly gatherings formed the foundations of the Bloomsbury group: 'Vanessa and I were in a twitter of excitement,' wrote Virginia. 'It was late at night; the room was full of smoke; buns, coffee and whisky were strewn about; we were not wearing white satin or seed pearls; we were not dressed at all.'

Those last six words. Woolf is using dress to mark this foundational shift in their lives. What she means by 'not dressed' is, clothes do not have to be a tool of social codification or control. The sisters were no longer mute onlookers and victims. They were protagonists.

It was a refusal of the clothes they had previously worn, and all they had endured. Young male guests, like Clive Bell and Lytton Strachey, 'criticised our arguments as severely as their own,' wrote Woolf. 'They never seemed to notice how we were dressed or if we were nice looking or not.'

Here, Woolf is connecting the rejection of societal dress codes with a new equality of ideas. Virginia and Vanessa created an environment where what they wore, how they looked, did not matter. They began to exist as human beings.

The young men in the group had studied at Cambridge at the time of philosopher G. E. Moore, whose 1903 work *Principia Ethica* asked, 'What is good?'. Virginia and

Vanessa had been denied equal education: they were home schooled and had attended 'ladies' classes. On Thursday nights, in their home, they engaged as equals.

Woolf remembered how the parameters of Bloomsbury opened up at an early meeting. 'Vanessa, having said perhaps that she had been to some picture show, incautiously used the word "beauty". At that, one of the young men would lift his head slowly and say, "It depends what you mean by beauty". At once all our ears were pricked. It was as if the bull had at last been turned into the ring.'

How did fashion change? Parisian couturiers, such as Paul Poiret, are usually credited with loosening the silhouette in the early 20th century. Yet in 1905, Poiret's designs still used corsets.

The young adults of 46 Gordon Square tell us a different story. Their rejection of society's fashion was interwoven with their radical conversations about ideas and philosophy. We can imagine other young humans around the world at the time taking similar action, ones out of the spotlight so their story is not told. Virginia and Vanessa's adoption of loose and dishevelled clothing was not fashion. The fashion of the time wanted them to stay corseted and silent. This was anti-fashion.

Anti-fashion does not mean ignorance of fashion. It takes sophisticated understanding to reject what you oppose with purpose and conviction. Woolf knew the power of clothing. In 1907, she began working on what would become her first novel, *The Voyage Out*. On the fourth page, Woolf defined the character Mrs Ambrose by writing, 'She knew how to read the people who were passing her . . .' and then,

'When one gave up seeing the beauty that clothed things, this was the skeleton beneath.'

On the ninth page, she clearly links fashion with the trap of the society they had escaped. She described a stultifying dinner, at which women acted accordingly. 'Each of the ladies, being after the fashion of their sex, highly trained in promoting men's talk without listening to it, could think – about the education of children, about the use of fog sirens in an opera – without betraying herself.'

Early drafts of the novel feature a plot of queer desire between the characters Rachel and Helen. Woolf cut the queer desire plot from the final version, thought to be an act of self-censorship. Female queer desire was not acceptable or even acknowledged within British society, let alone British literature. It was not until 1928 that Radclyffe Hall published *The Well of Loneliness*, considered to be the first lesbian novel in English. A British court found the book to be 'obscene'. Woolf was present at the trial.

Woolf could not write about what she wanted to write about. What she could do was forensically examine and skewer the society that stopped her from being herself. From the beginning, the language of clothing and fashion was at the heart of this project.

There are no known photographs of Bloomsbury group gatherings from these early years. In 1910, someone in their circle gets a camera.

Suddenly, we can see the liberating effect of what they had been doing. Here's Woolf in March of that year, wearing a knit coat in Studland, Devon. The long lines of cable knit emphasize the straightness and looseness of the garment.

The rib collar adds pleasing contrast. There is no cinched waist.

She had already established what today we would consider a Virginia Woolf 'look'. She would cover herself in garments that followed the line of her body, without cinching or exaggeration. She favoured pattern, in either print or texture, and wore dresses and skirts rather than trousers, without appearing overtly feminine.

The same is true of an image from a year later. Woolf is wearing a long-line dress with the busyness of print, flowing down to the floor: garments of summer now able to let in air.

I love this next photograph from 1912, of Virginia wearing a neat cardigan and long skirt, towering over her sister Vanessa, whose arms are thrown up in the air. By them is Leonard, whom Virginia married that year.

What life in this image! The freedom of movement and expression. The simple ease of the garments, gendered but with barely any real difference between them. This was more than rare pleasure.

Throughout her life, Woolf displayed symptoms that today could be diagnosed as bipolar disorder. Her life has often been defined by the unbearable lows: my paperback copy of *Mrs Dalloway*, from 1989, talks in the author biography of her 'recurring bouts of madness'.

This stigmatizing narrative of 'madness' has stuck. If we approach Woolf through her clothing, we can give her space to recover and find herself. Through this study we can treat those that experience mental ill health as human beings, rather than impose victimhood upon them.

For in Woolf's life, there could also be great highs. Those close to Woolf would describe her as the most glorious company. 'Mrs V Woolf arrived after tea to the great joy of the household,' once wrote the Charleston housekeeper

Grace Higgens, 'as she is very amusing, & helps to cheer them up.' Woolf knew joy.

On Monday 15 February 1915, Woolf wrote in her diary. She was 33, just over a month away from the publication of that first novel, *The Voyage Out*. As with her fiction, her diary at the time was still polite, tending to the surface rather than scouring deep.

The day before, she had written about the rain, cleaning silver. She had to repair some clothes. The entry ends, 'From all this, it is clear that I don't want to mend my dress: & have nothing whatever to say.'

Woolf had only been keeping the diary for six weeks. It was her first known attempt at keeping a regular diary since 1909. Suddenly, on this Monday 15 February, Woolf wrote 282 words that snap into searing focus. She wrote about clothes.

That afternoon, she had travelled into London with Leonard. 'I am really in rags,' she wrote. 'It is very amusing. With age too one's less afraid of the superb shop women. These great shops are like fairies' palaces now. I swept about in Debenham's & Marshalls & so on, buying, as I thought with great discretion. The shop women are often very charming, in spite of their serpentine coils of black hair.'

It would be ten years before the publication of *Mrs Dalloway*, in which she used fashion and consumerism as primary tools to conjure the stifling horror of London society post-World War I. This diary entry of 1915 is like an out-of-the-blue prototype of *Mrs Dalloway*.

'By the way,' she wrote, 'I met Walter Lamb at Dover

Street station – A gentleman in frock coat, top hat, slip, umbrella &c.' Lamb had proposed marriage to Woolf in 1910: she turned him down. A couple of lines later she wrote, 'His satisfaction is amazing: it oozes out everywhere.'

The day sparked her. 'Then I had tea, & rambled down to Charing Cross in the dark, making up phrases & incidents to write about. Which is, I expect, the way one gets killed.'

Clothing was close to the nerve. The entry concludes with the following line. 'I bought a ten & elevenpenny blue dress, in which I sit at this moment.'

Here is the diary, written in her own hand.

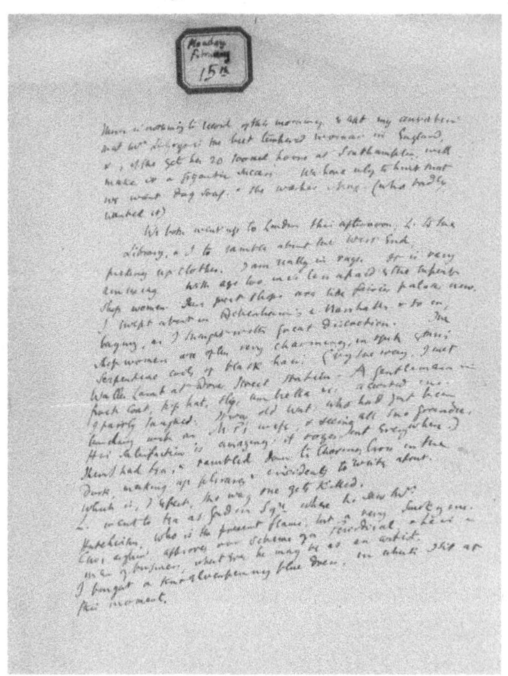

It would be her final entry for two and a half years. Woolf experienced her most extended period of mental ill-health, beyond her husband's care.

This double-exposed photograph is from the summer of 1916, spent recuperating in Cornwall.

When she returned to diary writing in August 1917, for months the entries are brief. No mention of clothes. She writes about the rain, the sun, butterflies, a hawk.

Her language of clothes rapidly evolved. This photograph was taken in 1917 by Lady Ottoline Morrell. Look at the checks in Woolf's outfit: a tight grid on the long skirt, then a wildly blown-up plaid on the scarf.

Woolf was building a sophisticated language of clothing. And yet she derided herself. On 23 June 1919, she wrote in her diary, 'I am resigned to my station among the badly dressed'.

Her clothing bothered her. She was about to publish her second novel, *Night and Day*. 'Why am I calm & indifferent as to what people say of *Night & Day*, & fretful for their good opinion of my blue dress?'

A dichotomy was revealing itself in Woolf: a disdain for fashion, yet a fascination with its hold. It is a dichotomy that I experience myself. I have written about fashion for over twenty years, but if someone compliments me on how I look, I'll deflect it quickly – there's a stain, I'm wearing it all wrong, I look like a schlub.

The other morning, I bumped into Andrew, who I've gotten to know from walking the dog. He asked about my work, and then he said, 'Of course I know nothing about fashion.' Andrew said it like it was the end of the matter – that he had never, and would never, know anything about fashion.

In terms of fashion industry, I'm sure he's right. Why would he need to know anything about fashion? But, like everyone, Andrew has an advanced knowledge of clothing. He uses a primary understanding of clothes to navigate daily life: the authority of police is expressed through their uniform; the power of politicians through their suits; his own appropriateness to integrate within a community; the agitation caused by someone disrupting codes to express themselves.

This knowledge of clothing is unconscious, like our knowledge of language. As with our knowledge of language, we are always learning. Our understanding of clothes is not finite, but is always evolving, and yet we tend to brush it off.

This dichotomy, Woolf's dichotomy, is at the heart of our contemporary experience with fashion. It is the tension between our self-denial and our subconscious knowl-edge. In conversation we act embarrassed, yet deep down we want to know more. We are drawn to tension. It fascinates us. If we can understand this tension, we can be released from it. Then, maybe, we can unlock our relationship with fashion.

Woolf's project was to cut through the layers, to find a way towards what felt true within the constrictions of a repressive society. The day after her 38th birthday, she set intentions for her work, for writing with 'no scaffolding; scarcely a brick to be seen', as if she wanted to disrobe her sentences and get to the heart of the matter.

And then Virginia met Vita. It happened at dinner on 14 December 1922. The next day, Woolf described 'the lovely gifted aristocratic Sackville West' as 'florid, moustached, parakeet coloured . . .'

The following undated photograph of Sackville-West shows her facial hair. I write that sentence specifically, because if I were to say, 'shows she accepted her facial hair', or 'had no problem with her facial hair', it would be perpetuating the patriarchal stance that female facial hair is abnormal and should be removed. It would become part of the amusement that has prevented Woolf's queerness from being taken seriously. How hilarious! So what? Sackville-West had facial hair, and Woolf loved her full-bodied, loved every part of her body.

The photograph of Sackville-West was taken at Woolf's home, Monk's House. On her lap is Sarah the dog. Notice the precise simplicity of Sackville-West's coat, and the patterned complexity of the fashioned chair on which she sits.

To Woolf, Sackville-West's moustache was an elemental attraction. It was another example of Woolf's disregard for societal norms.

A couple of days after first meeting Woolf, Sackville-West wrote to her husband, Harold Nicholson. Their marriage was open, both were queer. Sackville-West said of Woolf, 'She is utterly unaffected: there is no outward adornments – she dresses quite atrociously.'

Wait, Sackville-West just gave us eye-witness evidence that Woolf was badly dressed. Doesn't that wipe out my argument? No. Sackville-West was of the aristocracy, the part of society that profited most from adhering to dress codes.

Sackville-West and Woolf had already seen each other again. 'She was smarter last night,' Sackville-West wrote to her husband. That word 'smarter' is key – it carries a sense of acceptability. What was Woolf wearing that was smarter? Sackville-West continued, 'that is to say, the woollen orange stockings were replaced by yellow silk ones, but she still wore pumps.'

That sentence sounds like a styling decision taken today backstage at Prada. Woollen orange stockings, yellow silk stockings, pumps: these are gloriously twisted, so-wrong-it's-right fashion words. Why do they work? Because there is tension, wrongness, clash.

There is also vivacity. All these black-and-white photographs of Woolf as a young adult: how much less haunted, less doomed, more self-contained, more vigorous would they appear if we could see her as a brave human asserting her agency in these oranges, these yellows?

This photo of Woolf, relaxing on a sunlounger while on holiday in Devon, encapsulates this sense of being badly dressed/gloriously dressed.

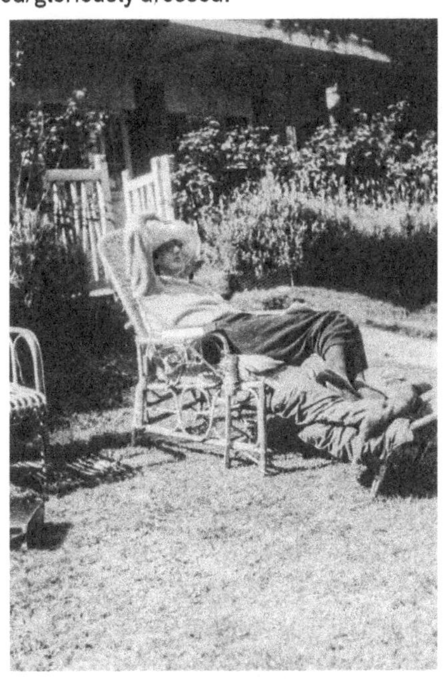

In June 1923, Virginia Woolf started writing *Mrs Dalloway*, initially called *The Hours.* 'In this book, I have almost too many ideas,' she wrote in her diary. 'I want to give life & death, sanity & insanity; I want to criticise the social system, & to show it at work, at its most intense – But here I may be posing.'

By 'the social system', she meant the patriarchal society that had limited and entrapped her. If she couldn't escape it, at least she could expose it.

'At once I feel refreshed,' she continued. 'I become anonymous, a person who writes for the love of it.' And then: 'I feel as if I slipped off all my ball dresses & stood naked – which as I remember was a very pleasant thing to do.' Note the plural in that sentence: 'all my ball dresses', as if she was still carrying the burden of each.

Again, she gave an analogy of going beneath the surface. 'To get to the bones,' she wrote, 'I feel my force flow straight from me at its fullest.' What was the barrier between the world and her bones, the flow of her force? Clothing.

Throughout *Mrs Dalloway*, Woolf uses clothes to depict the horror of society after war. She does so with different strategies, woven so deftly into the complex pattern of the text that they may not immediately be seen.

Most overt strategy first: Woolf crafts seemingly benign chatter about dressing for a party in the fashionable Westminster home of the protagonist, Clarissa Dalloway.

'Her evening dresses hung in the cupboard,' wrote Woolf. Clarissa picks out her green dress. 'She had torn it. Some one had trod on the skirt.' And then: 'By artificial light the green shone, but lost its colour now in the sun.

She would mend it. Her maids had too much to do. She would wear it tonight.'

The dress represents Clarissa, who is caught in a loveless marriage to an MP, her life one of vacuous social whirl. Her evening dress has the appearance of feminine sophistication and success, yet is torn and downtrodden, losing its colour. Woolf evokes Clarissa's loneliness and isolation by saying she will mend the dress herself, as if only Clarissa can mend herself. That night, she is hosting a party at home. She'll wear the dress, and carry on as if all is OK.

When Clarissa has a moment to herself, she takes the time to consider 'falling in love with women', doing so while 'putting her coat away'. She lingers, remembering the woman she loves, Sally Seton, who once 'ran along the passage naked'. The truth of her desires needed no clothes, but Clarissa cannot dwell in her naked truth for long. She pulls herself out of blissful reverie and into the anxious mundanity of dressing for the party she will host with her husband: 'Now, where was her dress?'

Running concurrent to this is the story of Septimus Smith, an ex-soldier and early volunteer for World War I, stricken with what was then called shell shock, now considered PTSD. Woolf uses clothing to show the banal horror of presuming that life can be normal in societies that allow for war. Smith reads *Antony and Cleopatra*. 'How Shakespeare loathed humanity – the putting on of clothes, the getting of children, the sordidity of the mouth and the belly! This was now revealed to Septimus; the message hidden in the beauty of words.'

Smith had married Rezia, a young hatmaker, in haste at the end of the war, billeted in Italy and fearing he had lost the ability to feel: '. . . scissors rapping, girls laughing, hats being made protected him; he was assured of safety; he had a refuge.' Woolf positions the handmaking of clothes as women's work and therefore a symbol of presumed matronliness, comfort. For Woolf, it is a false presumption.

The couple moved to London. Theirs is a life of stultifying torment: leisure, commerce. 'And there were the shops – hat shops, dress shops, shops with leather bags in the window, where she would stand staring.' And yet, to Smith, 'human beings have neither kindness, nor faith, nor charity beyond what serves to increase the pleasure of the moment.'

Woolf is explicit in her disdain, depicting commerce as what we do when we are not at war, 'for in all the hat shops and tailors' shops strangers looked at each other and thought of the dead; of the flag; of Empire.' That empire still covered roughly a quarter of the world's land area, claiming power over approximately 412 million humans, the vast majority people of colour.

And yet it was on the verge of puncture, the beginning of Britain's decline in economic and political power. In *Mrs Dalloway*, Woolf uses clothing and commerce to encapsulate the beginning of the coming fall. Clarissa is shopping on Bond Street, pausing in the window of a glove shop 'where, before the War, you could buy almost perfect gloves.'

This conjures a memory that goes beyond gloves, a memory which forecasts the decline of empire. 'And her old Uncle William used to say a lady is known by her shoes and her gloves. He had turned on his bed one morning in the middle of the War. He had said, "I have had enough."'

Woolf's interrogation of clothing in *Mrs Dalloway*, along with the blossoming of her love for Sackville-West, coincided with a flourishing of her own dress. Here is Woolf in June 1923, the month she started writing *Mrs Dalloway*, at Lady Ottoline Morrell's Oxfordshire home, Garsington Manor.

The lines at the hem of her dress, the floral swirls of the shawl, the puff of the feather on the hat: contrasts, tension, pleasure in dressing. It's that dichotomy again: the disdain for fashion in her written work, yet titillation in the act of dressing up. Rather than avoiding the dichotomy, she was embracing it.

A fortnight before the publication of *Mrs Dalloway*, Woolf got to the heart of the matter. That day, 27 April 1925, she had her second *Vogue* portrait taken at the studio of the magazine's photographers.

The experience of the shoot, or, as she called it, 'sitting', sparked in Woolf interrogative thinking. 'But my present reflection is that people have any number of states of consciousness,' she wrote in her diary. In the margin, she added, 'second selves is what I mean'. She continued, '& I should like to investigate the party consciousness, the frock consciousness &c.'

It's a statement of intent, but it's also a verbalization of thinking about clothes that had been brewing for years.

The *Vogue* sitting had been photographed by Maurice Beck and Helen MacGregor. Also at the sitting was Madge Garland, fashion editor of *Vogue* and lover of its then editor, Dorothy Todd. 'The fashion world at the Becks – Mrs Garland was there superintending a display – is certainly one; where people secrete an envelope which connects them & protects them from others, like myself, who am outside the envelope, foreign bodies.' Woolf defines herself as an outsider.

'These states are very difficult (obviously I grope for words) but I'm always coming back to it. The party consciousness, for example: Sybil's consciousness.' Sybil was Woolf's friend Sybil Colefax, a society host. She tried to encapsulate this consciousness in words. 'You must not break it. It is something real. You must keep it up; conspire together. Still I cannot get at what I mean.'

A couple of weeks later, she spelt out the complexity of her feelings about clothing. 'But I must remember to write about my *clothes* next time I have an impulse to write. My love of clothes interests me profoundly: only it is not love; & what it is I must discover.'

Woolf's relationship with Sackville-West had become physical. She was experiencing deep pulls of love. She wrote that her lover found her 'incredibly dowdy, no woman cared less for personal appearance – no one put on things in the way I did'. Woolf wrote of her lover's glamour, her full-breastedness, her voluptuousness: 'the grapes are ripe'. Sackville-West was on her way to Woolf's Bloomsbury home for tea. 'I shall ask her, whether she minds my dressing so badly? I think she does.'

Woolf took action. She asked Madge Garland if she would help her choose some clothes. Garland ordered for Woolf a long silk coat and dress from Nicole Groult, a Parisian designer, sister of Paul Poiret. Groult was lovers with the artist Marie Laurencin, and is thought by some to be the face in the rectangular frame of her painting *The Fan*. The face in the oval frame is thought to be Laurencin herself.

At the time, Woolf was musing on the nature of beauty. 'My own lack of beauty depresses me today,' she wrote on 3 March 1926. 'But how far does the old convention about "beauty" bear looking into? I think of the people I have known. Are they beautiful? This problem I leave unsolved.'

When the dress and coat were delivered, Garland wrote that 'Virginia looked supremely elegant in it and was so pleased and happy because its creation had not taken a moment of her time.' In May 1926, Groult visited London and met with Woolf to make any final adjustments to the dress. Garland wrote, 'At this fitting Virginia said to me, "If only you would always dress me I should have time to write an extra book which I would dedicate to you!" I wish this had been possible. A book dedicated to me by Virginia would have given me immense pleasure.' Woolf wore the dress and coat to a party given by Lady Ottoline Morrell at Garsington. A full-length view of the coat and its long, lean line.

Sitting down, we see the print of the frock, its vivacity.

Woolf doesn't write about the fitting, the frock or the party in her diary. Her pleasures, witnessed by others, are not admitted to herself. Perhaps this is the 'looking-glass shame', the lifelong trauma of abuse. Instead, a couple of days later, she records a humiliation. Clive Bell, husband of her sister Vanessa, had laughed at her hat. It had been chosen for her by Dorothy Todd, as had her dress. She tried to change the subject, but those with her kept asking about her clothes, thinking Woolf was in on the joke: 'it was very forced & queer & humiliating. So I talked & laughed too much.'

Once again she reveals how clothing was like a thin skin over her anxieties, her mental health: '& I came away deeply chagrined, as unhappy as I have been these ten years; & revolved it in sleep & dreams all night; & today has been ruined.'

In 1926, Dorothy Todd was fired from *Vogue*. Two days later, Madge Garland was also sacked, described as Todd's 'mistress' in the private diary of the magazine's managing editor. Todd threatened to sue over her dismissal, but the magazine's owner, Condé Nast, said if she did, he would 'defend himself by attacking Todd's morals', as in, her queerness. The women were ruined, shunned socially. Queer women could not live life.

Orlando: A Biography was Woolf's watershed. At the heart of the 1928 novel are two pages of philosophical writing about gender and clothes, text that can be lifted straight out of the book, separate from plot or narrative: 'there is much to support the view that it is clothes that wear us and not we them,' she wrote.

Woolf had the idea for the novel on 5 October 1927: 'a biography beginning in the year 1500 & continuing to the present day, called Orlando: Vita; only with a change about from one sex to another.' She wrote quickly, finishing the initial draft by March 1928. On the first day of June, it went to the printer. To celebrate, Woolf and Sackville-West pierced their ears.

By the midpoint of the book, Orlando has transitioned and is now a woman. 'The change of clothes had, some philosophers will say, much to do with it,' Woolf wrote. 'Vain trifles as they seem, clothes have, they say, more important offices than merely to keep us warm. They change our view of the world and the world's view of us.'

A few lines later, Woolf wrote, 'If we compare the picture of Orlando as a man with that of Orlando as a woman we shall see that though both are undoubtedly one and the same person, there are certain changes. The man has his hand free to seize his sword, the woman must use hers to keep the satins from slipping from her shoulders.'

A photograph of Sackville-West as Orlando, her satin slipping from her shoulders.

Woolf thinks there is more. 'It was a change in Orlando herself that dictated her choice of a woman's dress and of a woman's sex,' wrote Woolf. 'And perhaps in this she was only expressing rather more openly than usual – openness indeed was the soul of her nature – something that happens to most people without being thus plainly expressed.'

It was not prescribed ideas of clothing that determined gender, but something within. 'Different though the sexes are, they intermix,' she wrote. 'In every human being a vacillation from one sex to the other takes place, and often it is only the clothes that keep the male or female likeness, while underneath the sex is the very opposite of what it is above.'

Woolf's philosophy is clear: clothing is the only veneer that maintains the social construct of the gender binary.

Woolf was breaking through it on her journey into herself.

After Orlando, she was done with novels, or at least novels that took any traditional form. She wrote, 'I mean I think I am about to embody, at last, the exact shapes my brain holds.' Bye-bye binary, hello brain. Woolf had gotten underneath the surface, heading inside, towards understanding. She got so close. If only we could follow her.

If only she'd realized the potency of clothing earlier in her life. It may have prevented her involvement in an incident that rightly casts a cloud over Bloomsbury, which we will consider next.

The Dreadnought Hoax and the visual language of power

On 7 February 1910, a group of white British friends wore blackface and dressed in robes supplied by a theatrical costumier. They were pretending to be members of the Abyssinian royal family, 'Prince Makalen' and his court, requesting a visit on board HMS *Dreadnought*, the British Navy's flagship. *Dreadnought* was introduced in 1906, its technological advances – new turbines and bigger guns – ramping up the global arms race. Abyssinia is today called Ethiopia.

The stunt became known as the Dreadnought Hoax. It was the idea of Horace de Vere Cole, friend of Vanessa and Virginia's brother Adrian Stephen. Throughout de Vere Cole's life, he staged hoaxes and pranks. This photograph is of an earlier blackface episode, from 1905. It features Cole, in the centre, dressed as the uncle of the sultan of Zanzibar, who was visiting London at the time. Adrian Stephen is standing on the far left. The photograph is from one of the Monk's House photo albums, belonging to Virginia and Leonard.

In 1910, among the friends taking part in the Dreadnought Hoax were Virginia Stephen and Duncan Grant. Virginia is seated on the left, Adrian Stephen is on the right. Grant is standing on the far right.

At that time, the question of offence didn't even occur to them, so deeply did racism run through British society. If a 21st-century writer and artist were to dress similarly and wear blackface today, they would be cancelled.

On 9 February 1910, Grant wrote to John Maynard Keynes, his then lover. 'I suppose I must describe Monday's escapade,' his letter began, 'or you will be enraged that I left it to someone else to tell you.' Virginia Stephen and Grant were last minute additions: '2 of the sparks fell through at the last minute so Virginia & I were pressed to take their places, which we did.'

At seven o'clock on the Monday morning, 'Mr Clarkson's artists arrived & made us up in a marvellous way with beards & colour & wigs & what not', and they put on their costumes, as well as 'immensely long patent leather boots'. They 'bought an Abyssinian grammar, and a few hundred pounds worth of jewels.'

In today's money, £500 is around £75,000.

They telegraphed ahead and got the train to Weymouth Harbour, 'where we found a lovely young lieutenant in full clothes drawn up with a detachment of their jackets, saluting.' Clothing played its role in their pretense of power throughout. The party were taken out by boat to the *Dreadnought*, 'where we found a full regiment of marines drawn up on deck playing *Yankee Doodle*.' They were shown around the ship. 'Can you believe it?' wrote Grant.

A few days later, Cole leaked the hoax to the press. A front-page story in the *Daily Express* told all. It described the collective as: 'Five young men and one young woman, all of them extremely well-connected, and all of them well-to-do.' The piece went into detail about their costumes. 'Expenses appeared to have been of no account,' said the *Express*, 'and the ringleader actually took to the costumier books showing exactly what the princes should wear.'

The paper continued, 'Of course, they could have been fitted out in rough-and-ready fashion at an instant's notice,' but that Cole 'demanded accuracy of detail, and so some days had to be spent in procuring a rigidly correct make-up.'

When the paper described their appearance, it revealed the context of the times. 'The three young men and the young woman all had their hair cut short,' it said. The *Daily Express* then printed a line that featured the n-word. That word, on the front page of a British newspaper. It was part of everyday speech.

'Their faces, arms and hands were dyed to the proper hue. They wore turbans and flowing robes. Round the neck of each, suspended by a gold chain, was an Early Christian cross. Their persons fairly glittered with costly jewels.'

In their lifetime, and indeed into the 21st century, the hoax was mostly seen in a favourable light, or as a mild amusement, within white-dominated academia and media. They did not consider it offensive to people of colour. At the time, if anyone was seen as offended, it was the white naval officers on board the ship who had been tricked. Even in 2012, the UK paper *The Observer* wrote a news story giving new details about the hoax without once mentioning the offensiveness of blackface and cultural appropriation of clothing.

In his 1972 biography of Virginia Woolf, her nephew Quentin Bell wrote briefly of the hoax. He said, 'No one had the vaguest idea of what an Abyssinian, let alone an Abyssinian Emperor, looked like.' This ignorance is at the heart of the problem.

At the time, Abyssinia was one of the very few African countries not colonized by European powers. Britain had long exploited and oppressed African people. Britain's Royal African Company of the 17th and 18th centuries is said to have enslaved and shipped the most Africans in the history of the slave trade.

From 1870, Britain was part of what became known as 'the scramble for Africa'. At one point, Britain was said to have control of over 30% of the African population. Abyssinia retained its own sovereignty.

Colonialization was about racist power and making money. Authority was given to commercial associations, such as the Imperial British East Africa Company, founded and chaired by Sir William MacKinnon, a Scotsman.

A sculpture of MacKinnon once stood in Mombasa, Kenya. In 1964, the sculpture was moved to Scotland. It can now be found in Campbeltown.

Look at his clothes.

MacKinnon was depicted in the newly fashionable tailoring style, of sleek and sharp line, clear of unnecessary detail. Along with the late 19th-century wave of colonialization came the new tailored look of power, like that worn by MacKinnon. From its base in London it spread across all claimed territories throughout the world. This look of power was so successful, it was – and is – taken for granted.

Dressing as people from another nation seemed like benign fun, but really it was about power. Abyssinia was a place of resistance to colonialism. It's as if by dressing as Abyssinians, Abyssinians were finally colonized.

The Dreadnought Hoax was by no means the only instance of racialized dressing by members of Bloomsbury. In February 1911, the Friday Club – Vanessa Bell's weekly gathering for Bloomsbury group artists – held a Post-Impressionism Ball. It was to mark a major exhibition curated by the artist Roger Fry, which introduced the British public to the work of artists such as Cézanne and Manet. Guests were invited to come in Post-Impressionist fancy dress.

'We went as pictures by Gauguin,' wrote James Strachey to Rupert Brooke. Paul Gauguin is mostly known for paintings that depict indigenous people from what is now known as French Polynesia. Strachey was with Virginia Stephen and her brother Adrian, Vanessa and Clive Bell, Duncan Grant and Roger Fry. 'We were incredibly beautiful & very naked with a few brilliant clothes.'

In March 1911, Virginia wrote to her friend Molly MacCarthy, saying she might have to leave early from lunch because she had to 'dress up again as a South Sea Savage, to figure in a picture'. She ends the letter by saying, 'Was I less alarming as a savage, or as bad as ever?'

This was how they lived. Cultural appropriation. Blackface. Offensive language. It was normal to them.

We can try and make excuses:

- Virginia and Vanessa's grandfather, James Stephen, was a civil servant who drafted the 1833 legislation to abolish slavery.
- Vanessa Bell was said to be 'dismayed at the whole idea' of the Dreadnought Hoax.

- Leonard Woolf, himself once a member of the colonial civil service in Ceylon, wrote a book in 1920 against imperialism titled *Empire and Commerce in Africa.*
- Virginia Woolf helped in its research, compiling 800 pages of notes. For it, she found a quote from the book *Modern Abyssinia* by Augustus Wylde about England's actions that, she said, 'will not show one ray of honesty, and to my mind it is one of our worst bits of business out of the many we have been guilty of in Africa'.

But making excuses can compound the offence. Instead, we can look clear-eyed at the language and implications of their clothing. Fancy dress is not just frippery. It sends powerful messages. It reveals the power imbalances of its time. Offensiveness may not be understood until years, decades, centuries later. This does not diminish the offensiveness, because that era has shaped our own.

In the days following the Dreadnought Hoax, the press took particular interest in Virginia Woolf. 'Two interviewers have been today,' she wrote to Violet Dickinson, a week after the hoax, 'and one wishes for my portrait in evening dress!' It's an old newspaper trick that still works today: photographs of young women in pretty frocks sell papers, or, these days, get clicks. Nations were colonized, racism was consolidated, and then, within the colonizing nation, women were subjugated. This was the status quo that clothing helped to maintain.

Vanessa Bell

It was bugging me: where were all their clothes? There was just a shawl in the Monk's House archive; a couple of dressing gowns and a waistcoat at Charleston.

Kathy Crisp, the conservation cleaner at Charleston, suggested I read Grace Higgens's diaries, held in the Western Manuscripts collection at the British Library. Higgens had been Vanessa Bell's housekeeper from the 1920s onward.

Bell died at midnight on April 7, 1961. She was buried on the morning of 12 April at the church in Firle, the village to the west of Charleston. There was no service, no clergyman and just four mourners: Duncan Grant, their daughter Angelica, Bell's son Quentin and Higgens. In her diary that day, Higgens finished her entry, 'The Russians sent a man into space today, the first man into space'.

Four days later, on April 16, Higgens wrote the following: 'Had a bonfire & burnt Mrs Bells mattress & lots of her clothes, & pillows.'

Here was a clue. There are no clothes because the clothes had been burnt. Higgens gave no reason for the bonfire. Her diary entry is matter-of-fact, as if this burning of clothes was normal. Maybe it was for reasons of hygiene, maybe because they were just no longer wanted.

In her lifetime, Bell had a matter-of-fact attitude to what she wore. In the 1950s, she had old clothes turned into rag rugs that are still on the floor of Charleston today.

So many different garments combined to create something new: houndstooths and stripes and plain weaves, pinks and blues and yellows and browns and reds and greys.

Close up with the lushness of that repurposed cloth:

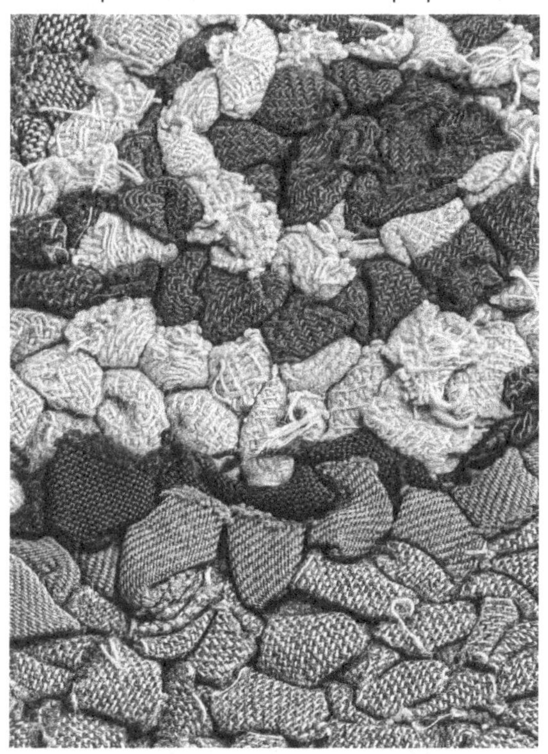

The rugs were made for her locally. It was part of a holistic philosophy of living that included making and mending her own clothes. I mentioned rag rugs to my mum. She said she had made them once. And yet, somehow, the tradition has fallen away.

From youth, Vanessa Bell had an intuitive relationship with cloth. Here's Bell, with her sister Woolf, play-acting with Jack Hills and Walter Headlam, on holiday in St Ives. It was

1892, Bell was 13. Hills would later marry their half-sister Stella, who died three months after the wedding.

That's Woolf behind, beckoning Hills with her finger. Bell is pretending to sleep on the couch, wrapped up in an expanse of fringed cloth. It is like an early premonition of how she would dress in adulthood, creating her own clothes that she often fastened with a safety pin. She has much to teach us about the pleasure, and the personal autonomy, that comes from making our own clothes.

In 1896, Bell started private lessons at Mr Cope's School of Art. All she wanted to do was draw and paint. She was 18. 'When I got into the grubby, shabby, dirty world of art students,' she wrote in an undated essay 'Life at Hyde Park Gate After 1897', 'I wanted nothing else in the way of society.'

Her half-brother George Duckworth had other ideas. Bell had to endure years of her youth under his control. 'How did we ever get out of it?' Bell wrote to her sister Woolf in 1908, four years after their escape to Bloomsbury. 'It seems almost too ghastly and unnatural now ever to have existed.'

At home, Duckworth abused her. In public, she was to be his society companion, against her wishes. If she tried to get Duckworth to turn down an invitation, he would deploy emotional manipulation. 'I was implored, begged with tears and embraces, bribed, cajoled', she wrote. If she continued to resist, 'I would find out after all that invitations had been accepted in secret.'

Duckworth turned Bell into his society plaything, preventing her from studying and making art. He gave her an opal necklace for her 18th birthday. The following year, Gerald and George Duckworth took Vanessa to Mrs Young's, a dressmaker at 65, South Audley Street in Mayfair. Two dresses were ordered, including one transparent black over transparent white, embellished with silver sequins.

'I remember that one well,' Bell wrote in her undated essay, 'for everyone then wore one dress many times, and though I felt all the thrill of putting on such a frock, still I came to dread the sight of it, so miserable were the many evenings I spent covered in the filmy black and white and sparkling sequins.'

In this undated and very staged portrait of the young Vanessa Bell, she is wearing a dress of transparent black sleeves over white. It could well be the dress she dreaded from Mrs Young's.

George Duckworth bought her the full wardrobe needed to impress in society, 'not only with dresses,' she wrote, 'but with jewellery, enamel brooches from Childs, terrible objects that were all the rage then.' Childs was a jeweller based in Knightsbridge. Duckworth also gave her 'fans and handkerchiefs and all sorts of extras that a young lady had to have.'

This wardrobe 'prevented the excuse that I had no clothes. Now when invitations came for Mr Duckworth and

Miss Stephen there was no adequate reason for refusing. Merely not wishing to go counted for nothing.'

In 1902, Vanessa travelled to Italy with George. The following portrait was taken in Rome in April of that year. It seems like the same dress. From its curved waist, we can see that the silhouette relies on a corseted figure created by stays. Bell was 23.

Around this time, Bell wrote an undated letter to her friend Margery, persuading her not to attend classes at the Royal Academy. In 1901, Bell had studied painting at the RA, taught by the artist John Singer Sargent. This letter reveals the reality of teaching available to women at the time, curtailed by their obligations, including to dress for dinner. It also puts the mending of clothes at the centre of a mind-numbing day, one that prevents an artist from getting the space they need to pursue their practice.

Bell told Margery that she would be able to paint at the RA between 9.30 and 1.15, but that she 'would come back & have a late lunch which you wouldn't eat much of because you would think, "In 2 hours I shall have tea" – you would then have to do mendings etc., see people, talk & tire yourself generally for 2 hours, when you would have tea – which you wouldn't eat, because you would think "two hours ago I had lunch" – you would then rush off to the R.A. do a very bad drawing, feel very ill, rush home, dress (untidily), & dine with the Tathams.'

In 1902, Bell had tea with a friend, Susan Lushington, in the garden of 36 Kensington Square.

Susan Lushington was nine years older than Bell. She would live a life free from marriage, described as 'eccentric' and 'formidable', two words that are often code for queer.

The pointless effort of the garments they are wearing, the excess, the hierarchical messaging, the waste of time. Some may find these garments appealing and wish for a return to such respectable times. I find the garments disrespectful. They are disrespectful to Bell, since all she wanted to do was wear her dirty painting clothes. When I look at the photograph, all I see is torpor.

Bell did not want to dress like that. Bell wanted to dress like this.

The photograph was taken in 1905, the year after her escape to Bloomsbury with Woolf, the year she would meet her lifelong friend, and sometime lover, Duncan Grant. Bell is natural in that loose cloth that forms her long-sleeve apron. It's only tied across the shoulder blades, all the hold that it needs. Look back at the size of the sleeves, the length that grazes the floor.

As we found with Woolf, there are scant images of Bell during the pivotal early Bloomsbury years, just that one of her at an easel. Why were there no photos?

Kodak invented the Box Brownie in 1888, the first ever camera with a roll of film. Before then, photography had been wet plate, such as the camera used by their great aunt, Julia Margaret Cameron.

Vanessa and Virginia entered adolescence just as photography began to be democratized. By 1897, the sisters had a box camera made by Frena. It was still an expensive hobby, costing around £1 for each new roll of film – around £130 in today's money. At first, the sisters were obsessed with the camera, particularly taking photos of their dog, Simon. By the early 1900s, their interest dwindled. The first years after they move to Bloomsbury: none.

Likely, they didn't have the money. But also, after their experience of abuse, maybe they were relieved to be no longer the subject of a lens. I put this to Hana Kaluznick, assistant curator of photography at the Victoria & Albert Museum. 'Photography is an incredible tool to subjugate people,' she said.

Today, it's natural for us to use images of ourselves as we assert our independence or changes in our identity, with every shift or rupture in our lives so easily recorded on social media. We take a pic, share it, and feel seen.

For the Stephen sisters, it could be that an image of their change was the last thing on their minds. What mattered was change itself, not recording what change looked like.

The first three years of Bloomsbury were chaste. 'The entertainment was frugal,' wrote Bell. 'I believe there was generally some whisky to be had, but most of us were content with cocoa and biscuits.'

She pointed out the gendered divide among the group before they gathered in Bloomsbury, a patriarchal split that played out along education lines. In her mocking words, we can see the elevated role that philosophy played in the education of elite young men, and Bell's determination to engage on the same terms.

Of course the young men from Cambridge were full of the 'meaning of good'. I had never read their prophet G. E. Moore, nor I think had Virginia, but that didn't prevent one from trying to find out what one thought about good or anything else. The young men were perhaps not clear enough in their own heads to mind trying to get clearer by discussion with young women who might possibly see things from a different angle.

Soon, everything loosened up. Vanessa married Clive Bell, a regular attendee of their Thursday evenings. Woolf would later tell of a pivotal Bloomsbury moment which, she said, had 'always lived in my memory' – though she added a caveat: 'I do not know if I invented it or not.' It was spring

1908. The sisters were sitting in the drawing room when in walked Lytton Strachey.

He pointed his finger at a stain on Vanessa's white dress.
'Semen?' he said.
Can one really say it? I thought and we burst out laughing.
With that one word all barriers of reticence and reserve went down. A flood of the sacred fluid seemed to overwhelm us. Sex permeated our conversation. The word bugger was never far from our lips. We discussed copulation with the same excitement and openness that we had discussed the nature of good.

A garment is at the heart of Bloomsbury myth. The dress's whiteness, culturally associated with purity and bridal virginity, heightens the sense of gleeful desecration.

Suddenly, they could talk about sex: queer sex, straight sex, all sex. 'It was, I think, a great advance in civilization,' Woolf wrote. What was Bell doing before Strachey spotted the semen? 'Vanessa sat silent and did something mysterious with her needle or her scissors.' Bell was making or mending.

Remember back in the Woolf chapter, we found that, around 1910, someone in their circle started using a camera. I think it was the Bells. The reason? Children. Julian was born in 1908, Quentin in 1910. Kaluznick's view is that, throughout the history of photography, 'the things people photograph are the same across the board: dogs, kids, their cars, lunch.'

In this photo from 1910, Vanessa sits in a circle of razor clam shells with Julian. In the background are Clive and the children's nurse, Mabel. In those days, people went to the beach fully clothed.

Vanessa's garments are still traditional, particularly the flamboyant hat, but her coat has a looseness, in contrast to the defined waist of the staff, as well as the cinched coats of a couple of women separate to the group, up the beach.

The photograph was taken on Studland Beach in Dorset. The beach huts are echoed in one of Bell's most celebrated works, *Studland Beach*, which hangs in Tate Britain. It was painted in 1912, by which time the garments of the standing figure had truly loosened.

The ambition and sophistication of Bell's art was evolving alongside the knowingness and freedom of her garments.

This next photograph is of Bell in 1913, but she could be wearing the deconstructed work of 21st-century Comme des Garçons. She was 34.

At first it looks like Bell is wearing a top and skirt, with some other garment tied round her waist. But look closer, and the off-kilter line of buttons of the top is of the same style and spacing as those in the bottom half. Its trajectory suggests the buttoning will meet in the middle, implying the top and bottom are actually the same garment.

The fabric that looks like it's wrapped is waffled, on a diagonal. On her right, it's at hip height, but the same fabric then comes round her left side and attaches under the buttoning. It's not a wrap, it's all part of the same complex garment.

The top is a puzzle. It looks like a separate garment, short-sleeved over longer sleeves that finish at a cuff. But this also could be trompe l'oeil, since the buttons that fasten both follow the same line from the skirt. The sleeves are wrinkled: it is clearly a favoured garment, worn often. The top part appears cut from all one piece, with no armhole seams. It is constructed by breaking the rules of construction.

Look even closer: what's that pointed tab of fabric that comes across the front placket on her left side, just above the waist? What is that panel of flat cloth in the middle that looks like it's tied?

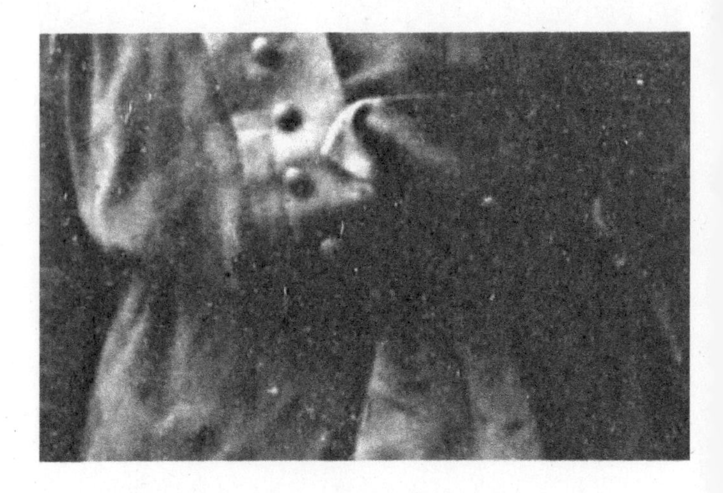

Complex garment, relaxed pose. It is an example of thinking through clothing, of the pleasure in complexity our minds experience day-to-day, hour-by-hour.

The same garment, seen from the side and sitting down. Bell is arranging flowers with Duncan Grant.

These photographs were taken the year that the Omega Workshops opened in Bloomsbury, founded by curator and art historian Roger Fry. Omega Workshops created furniture and fabrics with designs by young British artists. Woolf wrote of Omega Workshops, 'It was to be a society of people of moderate means, a society based upon the old Cambridge ideal of truth and free speaking, but alive, as Cambridge had never been, to the importance of the arts.' Bell and Grant were both directors and frequent contributors.

Bell was two years into a relationship with Fry. They were sexual partners and philosophical collaborators, their discussions ranging widely across art, colour, criticism, culture. 'How you have changed everything for me,' Bell wrote to Fry near the beginning of their relationship, 'all the things I most care for.'

Bell's rug and cloth designs for Omega Workshops pushed deep into abstraction, just like the liberated lines of her clothes, now free from the corset. She created this fabric design in 1913. It's called *Maud.*

At first, Omega Workshops just sold the printed linen. Then the cloth was also turned into garments, with dress-making overseen by Bell. This pair of pyjamas, in a different colourway, is a rare example. The pyjamas are now the property of the Art Gallery of South Australia in Adelaide, over 10,000 miles away from Bloomsbury.

The parallels between Bell's garments and her work continued. Here is Bell in 1914, photographed in Guildford, dressing with clarity.

This rug design is attributed to both Bell and Grant. It was made sometime between 1913 and 1915.

In the winter of 1914, Bell took a trip to Paris with writer Molly MacCarthy. 'She and I are going to revolutionize our dress,' Vanessa told Grant. On the same trip, Gertrude Stein took them to visit Pablo Picasso and Henri Matisse in their studios.

Abstraction travelled from Bell's design work to her art. This canvas, from 1914, is called *Abstract Painting*.

In April 1915, Bell wrote to Fry with the idea that 'I should make or at least superintend the making of several dresses'. The word was out. Lady Ottoline Morrell wanted one, and suggested that if Bell made several, 'they could have a sort of dress parade, perhaps in Ottoline's drawing-room and have a party to see them.'

Morrell wanted to hold a fashion show for Bell. 'I believe one could make dresses that would use the fashions and yet not be like dressmaker's dresses,' she wrote. Note the specifics of Bell's words – *using* fashions, not being part of them.

If the show ever took place, there is no record of it. But in 1915, Bell was photographed in a publicity image for the Omega Workshops, wearing one of her own dresses.

The image is black and white, this book is black and white. But her use of colour was wild and glorious. 'I am going to make myself a new dress,' she wrote to Grant in 1915. She asked him to bring her yellow waistcoat, then said, 'You won't like the dress I'm afraid, as it will be mostly purple'. There was more. 'Also I'm going to make myself a bright green blouse or coat, I haven't yet settled which'. Yellow, purple, green – bold colour fields, just like her abstracts.

When you put colours together, what you are really doing is playing with tension. Tension can be pleasurable, as some colours work together in harmony. Other combinations cause discord. Their placement, their saturation, their intensity: these are among the tensions that make art. We all deal with these tensions when we wear clothes.

In August 1916, Woolf wrote to Bell about the violence of her colour combinations. She writes about clothes that Bell made for their sister-in-law, Karin Stephen, who had married their brother Adrian. The tone is ironic, self-mocking.

'My God! What clothes you are responsible for! Karins clothes almost wrenched my eyes from the sockets,' she wrote, 'a skirt barred with reds and yellows of the vilest kind, a peagreen blouse on top, with a gaudy handkerchief on her head, supposed to be the very boldest taste. I shall retire into dover colour and old lavender, with a lace collar and lawn wristlets.'

Think back to that photograph of Bell from 1902, having tea with an 'eccentric', i.e. queer friend, both trapped in restrictive white dresses. Think of Bell's mind then, at 23 years old, stuck and wanting to express herself with garments that wrench eyes from sockets.

When Vanessa Bell made her own clothes, she is said to have favoured fastening them with safety pins. But Bell herself left little record of her sewing practices. It seems that to Bell, sewing and making was so normal, she didn't need to mention it.

I asked her granddaughter, the writer and historian Virginia Nicholson: how do we know about the safety pins? 'I think this comes under the heading of "family mythology",' emailed Nicholson. She said it was likely told to her by her mother, Anne Oliver Bell, or her aunt, Angelica Garnett, Bell's daughter with Duncan Grant.

'My mother was a very good and careful dressmaker who knew how to sew in zips and made her own hand-embroidered buttonholes,' wrote Nicholson, 'so she was probably affectionately critical of her mother-in-law's slapdash style of throwing clothes together.'

One morning, I was visiting the young designer Jawara Alleyne, a graduate of the MA course at Central Saint Martins in London. He has shown collections during London Fashion Week, and had recently made the human-size blunt worn by Rihanna on the cover of *Dazed*.

Alleyne's work is founded on reusing previously worn garments. He cuts them up, drapes them, reattaches them. He also cuts from deadstock material: bolts of fabric left over by other producers, which might otherwise be thrown away. For fastenings, he uses safety pins.

‘I’ve been using safety pins ever since I’ve been making fashion,’ he said. ‘You know, the idea of the renegade, of just pinning stuff together.’

We’d met to preview his new collection. As we were talking, something suddenly clicked: Vanessa Bell. I took this photo of Alleyne, with a long-sleeve T-shirt he’d cut with circles at the chest and sleeves, then safety-pinned.

Alleyne was raised in Jamaica and the Cayman Islands, where heat and moisture affect what you wear. ‘You want something you can slip into very easily and feel like you’re not wearing anything.’ Many of his pieces are made from simple squares and rectangles that can be put together and draped around the body.

I homed in on a sheer, swishy shirt. It was held together with pins.

It had a yoke across the back, the specifically cut piece on shirts that gives structure. It was clear that Alleyne could cut what's considered a traditional shirt if he wanted. But why should he? 'You get taught in universities how to design based on patterns that already exist,' he said. 'It doesn't have to be the shape that everyone cuts for a shirt. It's not just cutting patterns how you're told to cut them.'

It made me think about how far Vanessa Bell had come. Not only had she freed herself from the strictures of restrictive dress, she was also breaking ideas about how garments are constructed, and how they fasten, how they are lived in.

A portrait of Vanessa Bell by Duncan Grant, painted around 1915 or 1916. It's life-size, on wood, which suggests it could have once been a door.

In 1916, Bell urgently needed to find a refuge – a place where Grant and his lover, David 'Bunny' Garnett, could be employed on a farm, avoid jail, as conscientious objectors to World War I. She found Charleston. The house is set back deep from the road, at the foot of the South Downs, opening out straight onto lush land. Bell was to live there, with Grant, part-time, then full-time, for the rest of her life.

Making at Charleston was natural to Bell. She sewed curtains, lampshades, clothes. It was a constant practice. Grant recalled disturbing a conversation at Charleston between Bell and Saxon Sydney-Turner, a civil servant and member of Bloomsbury. Grant wrote to Virginia Woolf: 'I came in from the garden, and heard Saxon quietly saying "yes there are times Vanessa, when I think it would be certainly better to be dead than alive". Nessa made no comment and went on sewing.'

A portrait of Vanessa Bell by Duncan Grant from 1918, three years after the door painting. The dress looks the same. The location isn't noted, but since World War I did not end until November 1918, it's likely to have been painted that summer at Charleston.

Bell, at Charleston, in 1919, knitted fabric draped, doing little to conform to western European ideas about cut and silhouette.

An undated photograph of Bell, sitting outside at Charleston.

Another undated photograph. I love the way the structure of the cloth itself holds the sleeves open. The wonkiness of the horizontal stitched lines at the hips suggests it's at least handmade, if not homemade.

The simplicity of the outfit in this photograph from 1926: T-shirt-length sleeves, the headscarf, the Mary Janes.

In Vanessa Bell's time, the act of making clothes was a normal part of day-to-day existence for women in a heavily gendered society. Moves towards equality, industrialization, commerce and convenience have wiped out home-sewing; it's now a hobby rather than part of life for most women. For most men in western societies, it was never part of life.

It made me realize: why had I never tried? After all, Woolf wrote in her diary on 3 December 1921, 'I like clothes, if I can design them.' In March, I ordered some grey linen and a pattern. I borrowed a sewing machine from my sister, Sarah. The sewing machine then sat untouched for four months.

In May, my mum, Pat Porter, was hospitalized. Her kidneys had failed, caused by a previously undiagnosed blood cancer. It was swift and vicious. In June, she died. She was 77. She has always been, and always will be, in every word I write.

My mum was an artist, a painter who worked mostly in oils. She painted and sketched constantly, drawing right up until just over a week before her death.

She was also a maker. She sewed curtains, chair covers, quilts. She painted all over chairs, lampshade bases, walls. She knitted. As a young adult, she made and sold clothes.

Three days after my mother's funeral, I started sewing. I'd never used a sewing machine before. I watched a couple of YouTube videos, threaded it, got going. I was grieving through making.

Mum had given me so much energy from her anger at dying. Experimentation first: I cut a square from the bottom front of an old Hanes cotton crewneck T-shirt, my daily base layer. It was once white, now grey with age. I used this square to try out the machine, sewing random lines across it. The only thread I had was black, so the stitches were visible.

What if I tried to reattach the square? I pinned one side to its former home on the T-shirt, then sewed a new vertical seam, removing the pins along the way. The other side, the same. The square was attached to the T-shirt at both sides, but a letterbox shape had opened above, around the top of my belly. The effect interested me.

I had to pop out for something. I put on the T-shirt, wore it with a pair of shorts shorter than a handspan. There was a July heatwave, a digital thermometer on a billboard read

31 degrees. It was so cooling to have a letterbox of flesh exposed. Air could pass through. The tension in the garment had changed, a tightening caused by the two new seams, taking up cloth that had previously been unbothered. I sent this photo to my husband.

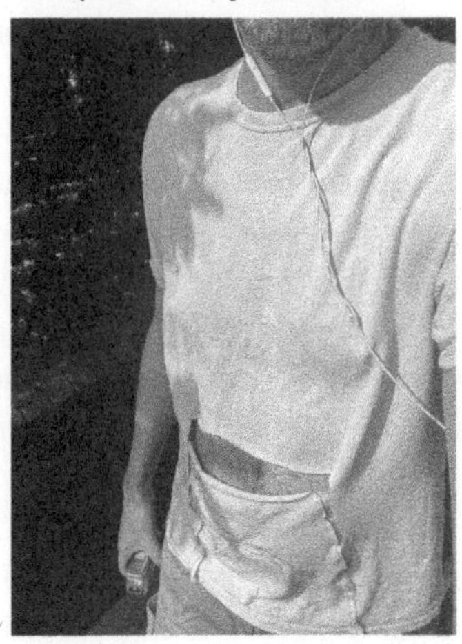

There was social tension, too. People looked at me, sometimes bemused, sometimes tickled. Some looked like they wished their T-shirt had an opening.

The letterbox was widening, the cut cotton giving, relenting. I took it off, went back to the sewing machine, and hemmed around its edge. Or, at least, hemmed as best I could. The stitches were occasionally wayward.

The next day it was set to be 33 degrees. I had to visit the bank. I wore the T-shirt again, the same shorts, sandals. The bank had no air-conditioning. There was a thirty-minute wait. I was grateful for my opening.

Afterwards, I headed to the British Library to read *The General Theory of Employment, Interest and Money* by John

Maynard Keynes. The security guards in the Reading Rooms can be funny about clothes: no coats, no padded gilets in winter. If they were going to object to my exposed letterbox of flesh, I was ready. I had some safety pins in my pocket. I could just pin up the hole. No need. They let me through.

And yet, I hadn't started making up the pattern I'd bought, to make a T-shirt from scratch. I realized the grey linen I'd ordered was too boring on its own. I was after tension, contrast. I ordered a metre of a linen in neon yellow check, some thread to match. The fabric arrived, but sat untouched.

Three weeks later, we had a rave. I needed something to wear. That day, at lunchtime, I got to work. To begin, I followed the pattern, cutting the front and sleeves of the T-shirt from the grey linen. For the back, I wanted something more. I cut the panel from the neon yellow check, extending the hem down 37 cm and curving it out to 17 cm extra at hip level on each side.

To construct the T-shirt, I started by following the instructions, sewing front and back together, first at the shoulder, then fitting the rib collar and the sleeves. I messed up often. I sewed the sleeves to the wrong side, zigzag stitching them secure before I realized my mistake, too late to correct. It meant the shoulder seams would have to be exposed. That was OK. I made like Bell, not worrying about supposed perfection. I like a wonky seam. I like a rough edge.

Before I stitched the side seams, I tried it on. With the excess at the back, it was in danger of being a tent. I pinned the back to encroach on the front, 17 cm on each side. I sewed it up. It felt like the front was being hugged by the back. The smallness and inward-pointing edges of the darker grey front created an optical illusion. It was slimming. The top had a strange tension, an individual presence.

My first finished garment.

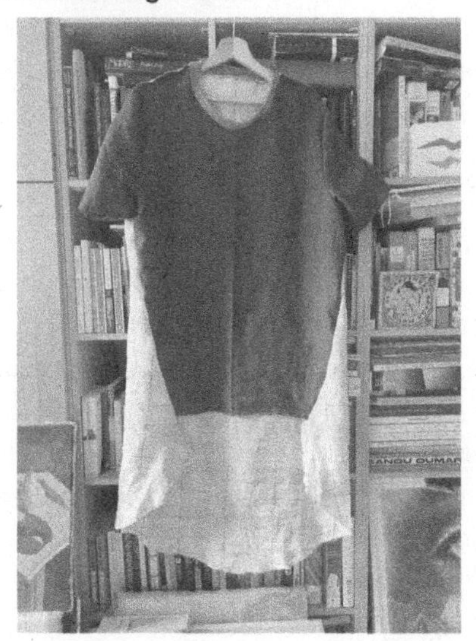

That night, I wore it to our party, Chapter 10. There were a thousand people in the room. Usually, I'd be a sweaty mess. The linen dealt with it all, wicking any moisture away. People kept asking me: who are you wearing?

It was my first dance since my mum died. I needed cathartic, elemental energy. Akua was playing, she'd come over from New York. Her bpm was at 142, her DJing about calm control, gently playing the hardest music.

It was 1.30 a.m. Linen is alive! It had bounce, like a jelly-fish around me. I could see the points of the neon-yellow back around the front. It was such a pleasure to have them in my field of vision. When I was dancing, they bobbled about.

I'd been writing notes in my phone through the night, so I could remember my thoughts. 'I would never have done this,' read one note. 'Thinking about Vanessa Bell has changed me.'

The next day, I ordered more linen, this time in plain, pale coral pink, and a check of blue, red and orange with touches of lime. When the order arrived, I used it to make another top. It's the same weight fabric, but the different colour contrasts give it a whole other tension. The grey front of the first top pulls everything in. The pale pink of this second top is open, at ease. It's like living on a picnic blanket.

Early the next morning, I wore it to walk our dog before the heat got too dangerous. I took this photo so I could see how it was working.

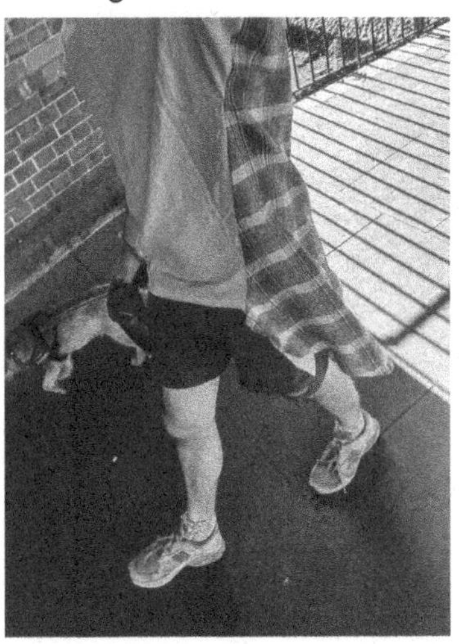

So much of this book has been written grieving, and making through grief. So much of this book has been written wearing clothes that I made myself.

Measuring wardrobes, or,
Where did they put all their stuff?

August. I was twisted round inside John Maynard Keynes's wardrobe. His bedroom is on the first floor of Charleston, a room he'd spend weekends in, sometimes weeks over the summer. It was next door to Duncan Grant's. The bathroom is down the corridor and round a corner. I was wearing my pink-fronted, check-backed top.

Charleston is closed to visitors on Tuesdays. The wardrobe is usually kept shut, but the Collections manager, Miriam Phelan, had opened it for me with gloved hands. I had my tape measure. I wanted to know its volume.

The wardrobe is stand-alone, up in the corner of the room. To my 21st-century eyes, it is tiny. Here it is, before Phelan opened the door.

The room is large, but much within it is small. Keynes's bed was single, 190 cm long and only 70 cm across. Google says that Keynes stood 2 m tall. His feet must have stuck out, the bed barely wide enough for him to curl up foetal. It is a bed for sleeping alone, no room for another human, for comfort, sex, embrace.

Inside the wardrobe is a hanging system of hooks, 18 in all: 12 across the side panels and six attached to the ceiling. Someone, at some stage, wanted something more practical, as a rail has been wedged in across the middle, held up by string attached to the ceiling hooks.

Phelan said that many visitors are shocked by the lack of storage at Charleston. Where did they put all their stuff?

The wardrobe was a tricky space to measure. I stood on the outside, then leant in and contorted my body round, taking care not to touch anything, to note the dimensions as accurately as I could. My body ached. I wish I'd kept up with yoga.

Each longer side at the back was 83 cm wide, with two shorter panels of 25 cm, and the diagonal front panel with the door measured 75 cm. The main body of the wardrobe was 160 cm high. There was then a shelf, 31 cm from the floor.

I only studied mathematics to GCSE. I got a B. I took that exam in 1989. A couple of days after my visit to Charleston, I did the maths using an online calculator. To work out the volume of this awkward shape, I cut it into two rectangles and a triangle. The rectangles were 83 cm x 25 cm, and then 58 cm x 25 cm. That left a right-angled triangle with two sides of 58 cm. I'd measured its longer side as 75 cm. The online calculator said it had to be 82 cm. Keynes would never have hired me as an economics assistant.

I wrote it all out in my notebook to make it look like I knew how to do the sums.

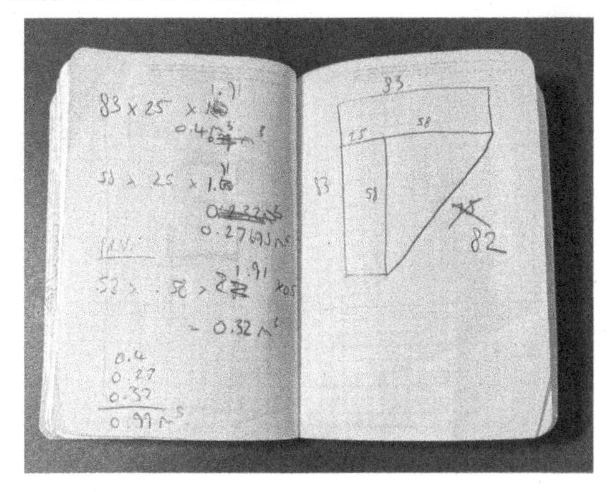

The total volume of the wardrobe is approximately 0.99 m^3. On the back of the door is some elastic, held in place by drawing pins. It could probably take the weight of ties, silk scarves.

There was also a chest of drawers in Keynes's room, with two top half-width drawers (50.5 cm x 42 cm x 19 cm) and then three full-width drawers (103 cm x 42 cm x 19 cm). That's a total approximate volume of 0.32 m^3.

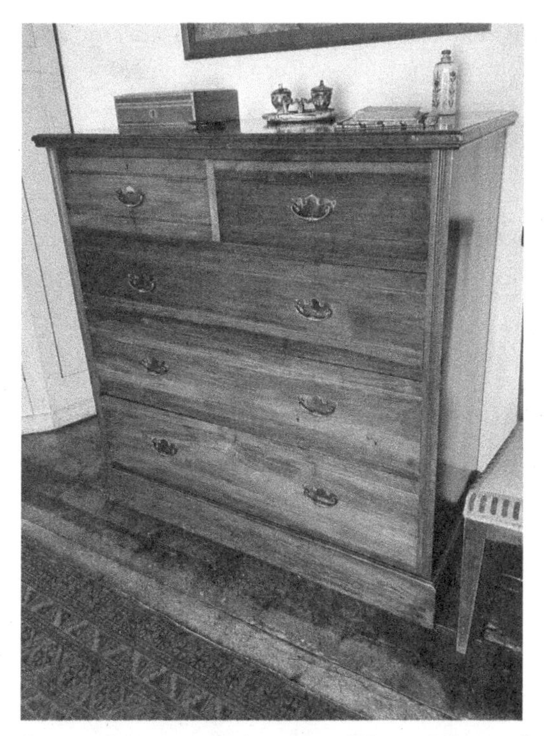

On top of the drawers is a copy of Keynes's bestseller *The Economic Consequences of the Peace*.

There is no wardrobe in Duncan Grant's room, though this doesn't mean there never was. Still in his room is a chest of drawers, with an approximate volume of $0.26m^3$.

In Clive Bell's room, there's a wardrobe of the same size and style as Keynes's – 0.99 m^3, and a chest of drawers with an approximate volume of 0.3 m^3.

For those three humans, that makes a combined total volume of 2.88 m^3.

Downstairs, in Vanessa Bell's room, is a wardrobe that used to be the cupboard for a fold-out bed. Its hand-painted doors are, to me, a joy.

There was also a chest of drawers in the room and, hidden behind a screen, another wardrobe, similarly hand-painted.

The bottom of the wardrobe is lined with a page from *The Times*. Newspaper in wardrobes is thought to help control humidity. The paper is dated 21 March, 1961: 17 days before Vanessa Bell's death.

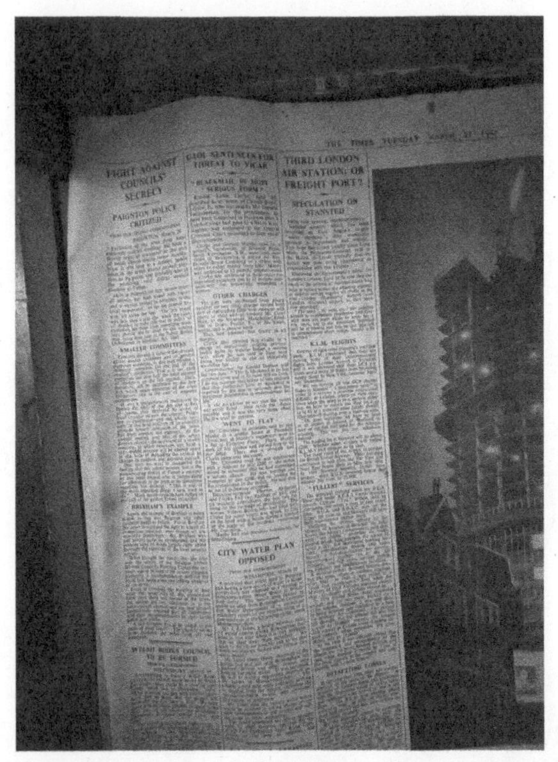
THE TIMES TUESDAY

FIGHT AGAINST COUNCILS' SECRECY

PAIGNTON POLICY

GAOL SENTENCES FOR THREAT TO VICAR

THIRD LONDON AIR STATION: OR FREIGHT PORT?

SPECULATION ON STANSTED

OTHER CHARGES

CITY WATER PLAN OPPOSED

After Bell died, Grant moved downstairs, taking over her room, as age lessened his mobility. He lived there until his death in 1978.

Across both floors, the bedroom wardrobe and drawer storage was roughly 4.05 m^3 in total.

Back home, I measured our wardrobe capacity. We live in a 1960s council block, a two-storey, three-bed flat that was converted in the 1990s into a no-walls, one-bed, open-plan affair. The bedroom is delineated by storage units, like a nest of wardrobes.

There are cupboards with rails, cupboards with shelves, and some drawers. A decent amount, nothing excessive. I measured the volume of them all. For two people, there was 4.42 m^3. That's more volume than Charleston, for just two of us.

When we talk about clothes, we can find ourselves thinking in our contemporary context: fast fashion, shopping as leisure, credit, disposable incomes. Fabrics today are light, often technical, easy to wear. We have washing machines in our own homes, tumble dryers, and the storage space in which to keep what we accumulate. Many people buy something cheap on a weekend, then shove it in a wardrobe and forget they ever got it. Or they wear it a few times, then bin it.

The size of the Charleston wardrobes provides a window onto a very different attitude to clothing. They didn't own that much. There was no high-volume turnover. What they owned, they wore and wore and wore. If they didn't wear it, they'd give it to someone else, or have its fabric used to make another garment, for themselves or for someone else.

Fabrics were heavier, scratchier. There was no central heating, so more layers were needed inside in cooler months. In summer, there was no air-con. Wardrobes weren't fitted: they were stand-alone. Clothing could be a pain, especially if life was lived adhering to uncomfortable dress codes.

But one resident of Charleston, recently vaunted by the fashion world, was more likely to have his clothes fall off, revealing flesh ready for pleasure.

Duncan Grant

'Come and sit by me,' said Kim Jones, the artistic director of Dior Men. It was a Thursday afternoon in June, less than 24 hours before his latest catwalk show. We were in the Dior Men temporary studio, a rented space in Paris just north of the Arc de Triomphe. Dior Men's success under Jones's watch means the show team is now too big to work in its atelier. Around us, Jones's next show for Dior was being finessed and finalized. It was a collection featuring the work of Duncan Grant.

Around 120 years had passed since the founding of Bloomsbury. Here was one of the world's biggest luxury fashion houses about to reveal new work centred on one of its protagonists.

'I didn't want it to be historical,' said Jones. His team had just been working on a top printed with *The Musicians*, a painting by Grant. The top was a pullover cagoule with a raised and slightly ruffled neckline, like an artist's smock.

Jones took out his phone and showed me a photo from an old collection of his from 2007. It was when he had his own-name label, not long after he'd graduated from Central Saint Martins, already a feted talent. I was at that show. He'd been thinking again about that collection.

The photo on Jones's phone was of a drawstring detail on a cropped jumpsuit, bunching the garment at the waist. Back then, Jones was attuned to a coming shift in what we wear: the move from formal to casual. Before Dior, he was artistic director at Louis Vuitton. He was responsible for that brand's collaboration with Supreme in 2017. It was a turning point, when luxury fashion finally recognized the casual way young people had long been dressing.

Jones is a Bloomsbury devotee and collector. Six months earlier, backstage before a previous Dior show, he'd said to me, 'I like things that change the world.' The Bloomsbury group were, he said, such people: 'outsiders who live and work how they want.'

Jones has a home in Rodmell, a few doors down from Woolf's Monk's House. He owns many works by Duncan Grant. But Jones had no interest in being literal in this new collection. It wasn't about copying a Duncan Grant look. It was more about expressing the freedom and possibilities of his way of being. Grant was a gay man at a time when homosexuality was criminalized. He lived floating above society, loving who he wanted.

Before a catwalk show, many designers are in chaos. Jones and his team run things smoothly, with only finishing touches to be done. We were sitting at one end of the studio, behind a row of desks. To the right were pinboards with photographs of each outfit, worn by its allotted model, and in show order. Down the other side were rails with garments for the show. At the far end, a painted seascape, in front of which was some fake grass.

Across the past couple of days of fittings, models had been dressed in a side room. When ready, they came individually into the studio and stood at the far end. Jones and his team would inspect the look, and the model would be asked to walk towards them, then back, just like on a catwalk.

'Let's make it more,' Jones said of one look. He didn't mean adding anything to the outfit. He was talking about increasing the tension, how the pieces related to each other.

A model entered wearing a tailored jacket with a sheer top layer, so the construction beneath could be seen. He posed, walked. He was holding something in his hand. 'We need to see the fan more,' said Jones. It was a Dior recreation of a fan that Grant had painted, with two kissing faces.

The fan was opened up, placed in the model's hand so it could be clocked by the audience and, crucially, the catwalk photographers. This is styling: the creation of an idealized version of nonchalance.

Jones was happy. Photographs were taken, both of the full look and then detail shots, such as the exact spread and angle of the fan so it could be recreated exactly for the show in 21 hours' time.

The team were finished. At 8 p.m., we drove to visit the show venue. It was a temporary construction in the grounds of the Val-de-Grâce military hospital, far south of the Seine. Inside the tent had been built a recreation of Charleston itself. Before it stretched a grass-covered catwalk made to look like fields of flowers. At the far end, a recreation of the

French seaside home of the brand's founder, Christian Dior, now a museum. Grant and Dior shared the same birthday. The catwalk's meaning: a walk from Dior to Charleston, and back.

It was Grant turned fashion. Repeating through the collection was a loose apron top, worn on one shoulder and falling on a diagonal. I took this photo of model Till Wenner in one of the looks.

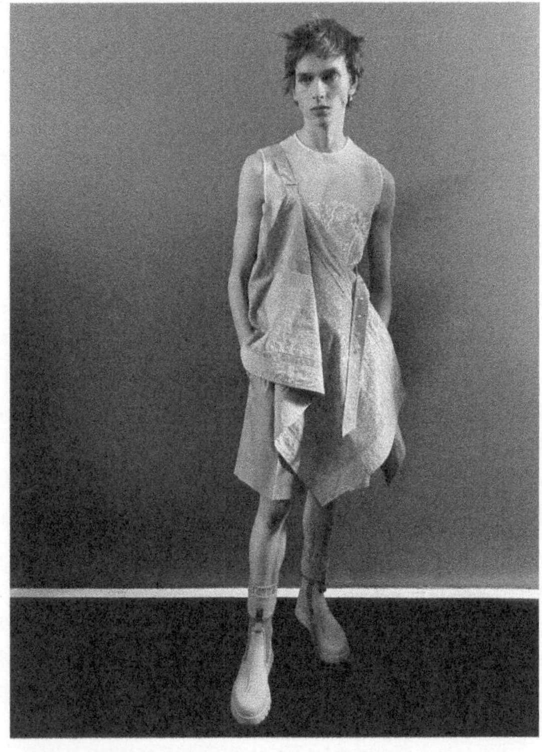

It reminded me of a photograph of Grant, taken by Vanessa Bell.

The pair were on holiday in France in the 1920s. Grant was painting in a field. Look close: he was wearing a vest, but had pulled the left side strap below his arm, creating a one-shouldered top.

It is gender-breaking. The amount of flesh liberated by the move was minimal. If he was hot, he could have taken it all off – Grant loved to be naked. Instead, he pushed one side down, which reads as a feminizing. He was 43.

Grant was an only child, the son of an army major. His family was that curious British combination: privileged and broke. His grandfather, Sir John Peter Grant, held the title 12th Laird of Rothiemurchus. Big words, no money.

During his childhood, Grant's parents were absent. They lived in India, leaving him at boarding school in England. Grant learned how to get along on his own.

Grant kept no diary in his youth, wrote few letters. Around 1902, someone took naked photos of him. They appear in the 1989 book *Private: The Erotic Art of Duncan Grant*, one photo from the front, one from behind. The book gives no context for the photos. Grant would have been 17.

And then he's there, memorialized in Lytton Strachey's paper 'Lancaster Gate', which recalls the Strachey family home, just north of Hyde Park. Strachey was Grant's cousin. He described coming home late one night, finding Grant asleep in his room.

'As I was getting into bed,' he wrote, 'I saw that all the clothes had rolled off Duncan – that he was lying, almost naked, in vague pyjamas – his body – the slim body of a youth of nineteen – exposed to the view.'

Notice the passivity – Grant's clothes 'had rolled off' – like it was impossible for them to stay on. Grant was 19, the year was 1904. Nineteen years earlier, Parliament had passed the Criminal Law Amendment Act, which criminalized sex between men.

'I was very happy,' Strachey continued, 'and, smiling to myself, I wondered why it was that I did not want – not want in the very least – what the opportunity so perfectly offered, and I got into bed, and slept soundly, and dreamt no prophetic dreams.'

A year later, Strachey and Grant became lovers. Strachey was five years older.

Strachey was jealous of Grant's friendship with his brother, James Strachey. 'Dearest Jambeau,' Grant wrote to James in November 1905, using his family nickname, 'I will send your bag and coat soon, damn your eyes why the devil don't you look after your bloody property you ____ cow.' I can't read Grant's handwriting to ascertain the exact type of cow. Maybe it's blasted? Grant was 20, James was 18.

In the British Library is an undated telegram from Grant to James. It was addressed to him at Trinity College, Cambridge, where he studied from 1904–1909. Grant wrote three words: 'damn dress clothes'.

In 1908, Grant began a relationship with John Maynard Keynes, who was studying at King's College, Cambridge. 'Dearest Duncan,' Keynes wrote on 10 July, 'Why aren't you a Cambridge undergraduate, damn you, instead of a wretched Londoner? Come, and I will make King's chapel into a studio for you and you shall paint all the beauties of the age and live on salmon mayonnaise, while Justin shall wait on you and Rupert shave you and Gerald tie up your bootlaces and I shall kiss you and we shall live happy and virtuous for ever.'

The roles of master to servant, particularly in the act of dressing, are presented here as a come-on. Other times, their letters about clothing are mundane. On 24 July, Keynes wrote to Grant, 'I found in the end your coat as well as other clothes and have left them packed in a brown paper parcel on my desk.'

Photography aided their relationship. On 28 July, Keynes wrote to Grant, 'I was very glad to get the photograph – you're dreadfully brushed up and I want to smooth your hair down Roman-emperorwise,' before saying, 'Dear, dear Duncan I love you very much and you're not here and I can only invite you.' Here is the photo, his hair in need of being made Roman-emperorwise. On the back it says 'J.M. KEYNES from D. GRANT 1908 July 27th'. It is mounted on card, a professional shot.

Grant's clothing was eroticized in Keynes's memory. 'Dearest Duncan,' he wrote on 9 August 1908. 'Oh, I've got a third vision of you – in a dinner jacket and a black tie enthroned in the little room at the top of the steps in Fellows Road as I entered from the street.'

In an undated letter from Grant to Keynes, a mention of clothing reveals the tensions, dangers and subterfuge of the time. It reads as if Grant and Keynes had been together, separating quickly to keep up appearances.

'Dearest Maynard,' Grant wrote. 'I do hope you felt

better after you had eaten some food. I hurried back & had 1 minute to dress in & managed it. There was a violent knocking at the door half way through dinner & mother said "Is this Keynes come for some more food?".'

He continued, 'Dearest Maynard, we mustn't often behave like we did today, it is too exhausting for our nerves.'

By spring of 1909, Grant and Keynes were more friends-with-benefits than boyfriends. They continued to correspond. In an undated letter from 1910, Grant wrote to Keynes about the bounty from a funeral. It shows his attitude to clothing: he wore stuff picked up along the way. 'It was luckily a lovely day and I was given a superb green ulster, practically new,' he wrote – an Ulster is a raincoat with a mini-cape attached, 'with yellow buttons which belonged to the deceased! also several suits of clothes.' Grant would also get painting materials.

In June, they holidayed together in Greece. Keynes photographed Grant naked. Grant told Keynes he could share the photographs with his friends, but only from a certain angle. 'You may show any of the back views to your friends – intimates – if you like as long as you do not let them know on any account who it is – you must say that it was a shepherd or something & that no one wears clothes in Arcadia. As for the front view I cannot on any account allow it to be shown to anyone.'

That same year, Grant painted a self-portrait wearing a turban. He is face-on, but the camp of his arm gesture suggests that Grant sees himself in costume, or fancy dress, appropriating garments from other cultures. Note his nakedness, the garment only accentuating his flesh.

Meanwhile, Grant's friendship with Vanessa Bell was developing. They had met in 1907. On 3 November 1909, Bell wrote to Grant, asking if she could call him by his first name. She continued: 'Will you dine with us on Tuesday next the 9th at 8 o'clock?' There was further information. 'It will not be a party so don't trouble to dress unless you like.'

Remember that camera? The one that appeared around 1910, which I suspect began being used by the Bells to document their children? Soon, there was unfettered photography. The following photos were taken at Asheham, where Virginia Woolf moved to in 1912. They are undated, but Grant visited that year, and in the images he appears young. They were in Vanessa Bell's photography album, so it is presumed she was behind the lens.

This next image seems from the same film.

Another undated photograph of Grant at Asheham shows the insouciance of his attitude to clothes. The shirt is a mere covering. The tie has a rude, liberated aggression, knotted with vigour to a length disrespectful to society.

Grant's discarding of clothes was already the subject of gossip. In January 1911, James Strachey wrote to Rupert Brooke to spill the tea. Strachey had been at a drinks party when Keynes arrived late 'in his shiny dresser', presumably his dinner suit. 'There was a most unpleasant story (in confidence of course) about Duncan's latest debauch. The duc de Condé was in London, & asked him to the rooms of a friend of his – a Mr Workman (late of Trinity apparently, an ex-friend of Dent's). It was after the theatre and the room was very richly furnished in the Turkesque style. The three of them sat and drank champagne for hour after hour, and Duncan has only a misty recollection of the rest. But he remembers that at the Duc's instructions, he and Mr Workman took off all their clothes and copulated on the floor, while the Duc sat watching them and "tossing himself off" – and explaining all the time that this was the latest vice – "Mixoscopy".'

In August 1913, Grant, Keynes and friends went on a camping trip to Norfolk. Bell was on the holiday too, but stayed in a farmhouse nearby. She took this photo of Grant, his shirt hastily buttoned. Its pushed-back collar makes it seem like the shirt could fall off any second.

On 28 July 1914, World War I began. Young men who enlisted in the army were given a prescribed set of

garments. '3 handkerchiefs', reads a document in the papers of Rupert Brooke, poet and sometime friend of the Bloomsbury group, '2 thick drawers; 2 flannels; 4 pair socks; 1 silk; 1 no3 jumper; 2 pair trousers; 2 pair boots; 1 gaiters; 1 oilskin & sou'wester; cap & band; great coat.' Brooke enlisted at the outbreak of war. He died of septicaemia in April 1915.

Here, I had planned to show you a particular photograph of Grant and Garnett, taken in 1915. It is kept in the Tate archives, in Vanessa Bell's photo albums. Unfortunately, it is now too fragile to reproduce.

In it, Duncan Grant looks into the lens of the camera. He's wearing a three-piece suit: jacket, buttoned up waistcoat, tailored pants. There's some sort of patterned shirt, buttoned up, maybe also a bow tie, or a tie tied badly.

His arm is around Garnett, who that year turned 23 years old. Garnett's arm is round Grant's back, and he is looking at Grant. Garnett is wearing a shirt, tie and what looks like the lapel of a jacket. It can barely be seen because, over the top, he is wearing an imposing military greatcoat.

It is double-breasted, with at least four rows of buttons. On the side of the left arm is a circle, on which can be seen some form of insignia. These are two men who were in love; two men who refused to go to war. Often in history, pacifists, protesters and anarchists have purposely worn the clothes of war, such as American anti-Vietnam war protesters in the 1960s and 70s, or British punks of the 1970s.

In January 1916, the Military Service Act was passed and

conscription was introduced. All single men aged between 18 and 41 were liable to be called up. This was extended to married men a few months later.

The Act made provision for those who objected to fighting if they agreed to do 'work of national importance', such as farming, or to be conscripted into a non-combat corps. Conscientious objectors who agreed to neither were imprisoned.

Garnett and Grant were conscientious objectors. They first rented a farm in Suffolk in the hope of avoiding conscription, but the Pelham Committee, which granted exemption from combat, would not agree to them being self-employed, presumably because this meant no one was overseeing them. It was only when Bell found Charleston, and paid farm work for them nearby, that the couple were safe. At Charleston, Grant and Bell and Garrett lived an intense, interconnected life, free from war, free to explore their sexuality.

In 1919, Virginia Woolf recorded an encounter with Grant. They were in London. 'Duncan passed through – a strange shaggy interlude,' she wrote. Grant ate a brioche, had coffee, chatted.

'Somehow, too soon, he hoisted himself into an astonishing long straight black coat, like a non-conformist ministers, hitched down his red waistcoat, & started off in a vague determined way to Victoria Station.'

The seclusion of Charleston brought liberation. An undated photo of a naked male model, in the garden. It was taken in a secluded spot outside Grant's studio, with a small square-shaped plunge pool for cooling off.

In the autumn of 1921, Grant and Bell went to live for a few months in the south of France. They were joined by their new housekeeper, Grace Germany, who would turn eighteen on the trip, and Nellie Boxall, who would become one of Woolf's servants.

The party went swimming in St Tropez, 'after which Nellie and I going into a little hut to dress, turned Mr Grant out' wrote Germany in her diary on 23 October, 'the poor man having left his trousers inside, had to trot about with his shirt, safety-pinned between his legs, to prevent it blowing up.'

Those safety pins!

Grant's way with clothes continued to amuse her.

'After dinner Nellie & I went to the Pictures,' she wrote on 12 November. 'Mr Grant went too, and, as it rained, he borrowed Julians overcoat,' Vanessa Bell's son Julian was 13 at the time. 'I do not think I ever laughed so much, as it reach[ed] not quite to his knees, & fitted him so tightly around the waist, so as to show off his figure as if he wore corsets, & the sleeves reached to his elbows.'

Back at Charleston, Virginia Woolf visited one August day in 1922. 'Then Duncan drifts in,' she wrote in her diary, saying he was 'incredibly wrapped round with yellow waist-coats, spotted ties, & old blue stained painting jackets. His trousers have to be hitched up constantly. He rumples his hair.'

A photo of Grant from 1923 shows his play with garments. He's in an otherwise sober suit, no tie. On his head is some sort of cloth, echoing the turban self-portrait of thirteen years earlier.

More from the diary of Grace Germany, this entry written at Charleston on 3 September 1924. 'Duncan Grant the artist thinking to frighten us dressed up in some weird clothes, and hobbled about, Louie thought he was a cow, Mrs Bell was very amused, also were Julian & Quentin.'

Grant continued to seek self-expression through clothing. In this undated photo with Vanessa and Clive Bell, he wears a collarless jacket that, to contemporary eyes, looks more like the neckline of womenswear Chanel. Its pointed pockets show that it is a military jacket: a pacifist once again wearing a garment of war. The Bells look as though they are relaxing into middle age, but Grant is still sprightly.

Grant, near-naked, no location, thought to be taken in 1925 or 26. We'd need him to stand up to see what was going on, but it looks like he's wearing super short shorts, cut offs, or a repurposed garment, maybe a shirt turned into bottoms; whatever, it is barely being held in place by that button.

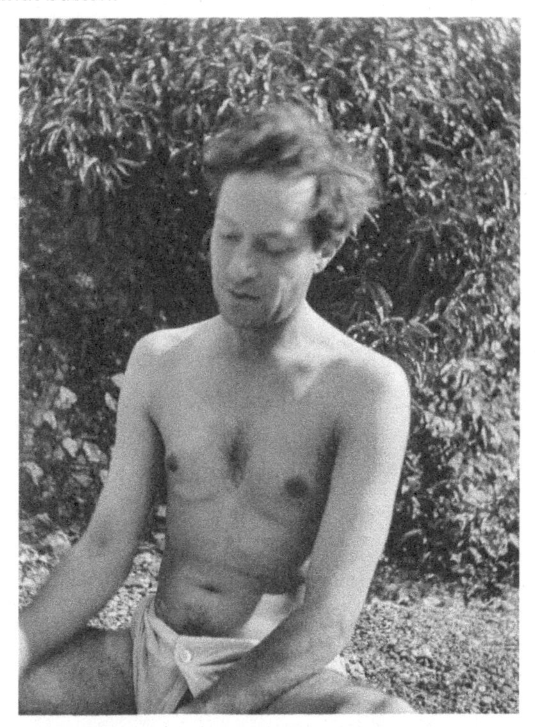

Grant painted male nudes throughout his career, both naked portraits suitable for public eyes, and unencumbered erotic art for private viewing. To paint, Grant would repeatedly wear the same garment.

This high buttoning jacket, with neat little Tyrolean lapels, themselves held down by buttons, was a favourite. Here he wears it in 1927. To his left is Angelica, his daughter with Bell, who was born in 1918. When this photograph was taken, Angelica did not yet know she was his daughter.

In 1927, Grant and Bell bought a house together in Cassis, France, where they could paint, relax, invite guests. Carrington took the following photograph of Bell and Grant. It's the same jacket, just a little bit filthier. It's covered in paint. Look at the slippers!

Grant, four years later, in Cassis, the jacket now gloriously dirty.

Grant was in his sweet spot. He was selling paintings. He and Bell had constructed a co-habiting relationship of togetherness beyond sex. He had a succession of male lovers, often overlapping. He had homes in London, Charleston, Cassis. This was contentment.

At 13.52 on 24 June 2022, three models were backstage, eating. They were sitting on stools, at a high round table, a buffet to the side. It was 38 minutes before the Dior show was due to start. 'Guys,' said a show producer, who was walking past and wearing a headset, 'It's time to go to the dressing.'

Some of the models were in black robes with 'DIOR' on the back. Others were yet to get undressed. In their own clothes, male models often remind me of kids interrailing. It was like they were at a station café, waiting for a connection. They loitered, finished their food, young men reluctant to shake off adolescence.

The backstage of the tent was curtained off into specific areas. Kim Jones had his own room. There was an area for hair and make-up. Manicurists sat ready. Models had their own hang-out space, and then there was the dressing room itself.

Models started to put on their clothes, aided by dressers where necessary. One put on a pair of shorts. Then his dresser put a white net on his face, while others lifted a sweater over his head. The net, and their care, was to prevent make-up dirtying the sweater, a hand-knit reproduction of a landscape painting by Grant.

At the corner of the room was a curtain. This led out to the line-up area, where models waited before their catwalk turn. Just behind the curtain stood Lucy Beeden, Jones's design director, and Melanie Ward, the stylist of the show, as well as the milliner for Dior, Stephen Jones, all there to give each dressed model the once over.

At 14.11, a model came out of the dressing room for his inspection. He was wearing a reflective zip-up printed with a lily pond design by Grant, originally for the Omega Workshops. The zip was fastened to a high neck. Its pull was of shiny metal. Beeden took out a cloth and polished it. There were to be no fingerprints on the catwalk.

I wandered up some steps to a long passage where the dressed models were milling about, lined up against the wall either side. The invite said the show would start at 14.30, but by then half the models weren't ready backstage, and no one was panicking. Fashion shows are like going to the cinema: the ticket says one time, but you must add around 22 minutes for the actual start.

By 14.37, I was getting twitchy. I've been to hundreds of fashion shows over the past twenty years. I know they always start late. I could see the Dior team weren't ready. And yet . . .

My seat was only a couple of minutes away from where I was standing, but to get to it would mean going through the catwalk entrance like I was walking in the show. Not a good look. I headed out from the backstage, went round the vast temporary structure, and entered through the front.

The audience was filling up, sitting on banked seating turfed with grass, everyone given a cushion to prevent stains. I didn't have my ticket on me, so went in through the wrong door, at the far end from my seat. It meant I had to go past the entire front row. There were Justin Timberlake and Jessica Biel. Sitting on his own was Jack Dorsey, the founder of Twitter. He looked startled, his posture correct, more upright than the usual slump of those who are used to attending shows.

I found my seat.

The show began.

It was glorious. Here is another of those lop-sided tops.

At the end, Jones took his bow. He was wearing a version of the top featuring the print of Grant's lily pond.

Afterwards, I headed backstage. The Dior team were clapping, cheering, hugging. It was a moment of release.

I went deeper to watch the well-wishers. There came Timberlake and Biel, there came Naomi Campbell, with Wizkid. They were all looking for Jones. They were out of luck. He'd left already, a long-planned quick exit, away to Egypt, and escape.

Catwalk shows thrive on possibilities and suggestions for how we could be in the future, often pushing at the gendered boundaries of garments. Within the bubble of fashion, this work can seem dynamic, world-changing, like how Charleston can feel when you are inside its grounds. But in wider society, the gendered language of clothing is still entrenched.

Two key Bloomsbury protagonists give us the chance to study men's clothing from different angles: as a means of repression, and as a means of assuming power. But first, we'll spend some time among a male secret society that gave so much inspiration to Bloomsbury. In doing so, we'll discover a surprisingly enlightened 19th-century attitude to gender, patriarchy, and clothes.

The Apostles, and conversations about style

One Saturday evening in 1888, Roger Fry presented a paper to the Apostles, an all-male secret society at Cambridge University. He was 21, studying at Trinity College.

The Apostles, formally known as the Conversazione Society, had been meeting for debates on Saturdays since 1820. Each week, a paper was presented, then discussed. They ate sardines on toast, a snack they called Whales. They drank coffee.

A rare photograph of Apostles, from 1876. Once an Apostle, always an Apostle: you could continue attending beyond your university days. That older guy has prime position between those two younger Apostles' spread legs.

Membership was by invitation only. Prospective Apostles, when being scouted, were called Embryos. Future members would include E. M. Forster, John Maynard Keynes, Lytton Strachey, Leonard Woolf. The philosopher G. E. Moore – Bloomsbury's 'prophet' – was an Apostle.

A photo from the Woolfs' photo album, captioned 'Moore'.

Fry's 1888 paper was titled 'Shall we wear Top Hats?' A top hat had become part of standard daytime dress for middle- and upper-class men in the 19th century, a tradition that continued well into the 20th. This image, by Swiss American photographer Robert Frank, was taken in the City of London, a financial district, in 1951.

Here is the first page of Fry's paper.

2/6

SHALL WE WEAR TOPHATS?

Now when I say top hats I do not wish to be understood to refer exclusively to that hollow ~~excrescence~~ erection covered by black plush which a large number of highly civilized men delight to balance on their heads. I contemplate also that spiritual tophat which covers not one part but the whole ~~entity~~ individual keeping it safe say its worshippers alike from the excessive rigours of philosophy & the enervating heats of religious ardour – safe in an equable and ~~satisfactory~~ temperate element of ~~the commonplace~~ convention. Safe alike say the scoffers from the breezes of nature & the sun of sympathy – but the scoffers ~~they~~ generally become poetical and must be discounted accordingly.

In it, Fry uses the top hat as an analogy for white male power. This top hat covered not just the head, but 'the whole individual', protecting the 'large number of highly civilized men' who wore them from 'the excessive rigours of philosophy'. Wear a top hat, consolidate your power, don't let anyone question anything.

Fry goes on to ask, 'Is the soul more than raiment'. There is no question mark in his sentence. 'Raiment' is another word for clothes. He's saying, is the soul more than clothes.

A few lines later, a paragraph is crossed out. 'And herein lies if we look for it the truth of the doctrine – that so many men care about raiment and so few about the soul.'

Fry qualifies further. He didn't mean raiment that's just for keeping the body warm, 'but that which society imposes on the individual members composing that society for no other reason than that it has the whim to do so.' i.e. the top hat.

At one point in the talk, he addresses the top hat directly, as if the top hat represents an entire crippling society.

Hear I pray thee the prayer of this thy humble servant and thine incomplaining footstool. And if it be possible grant to me of thy mercy some remnant of individuality some breath of air that I be not suffocated altogether beneath thy weight. Or at least I pray thee that I may have some short resting space before thou descendest altogether upon me & I be no more seen.

At the end, Fry states that he is not seeking a replacement for the top hat: we should not resist 'any particular convention that we object to' by 'replacing it by an another'.

Instead, he says, we should replace 'the conventional by a rational attitude of mind'.

Fry was not suggesting a new way of dressing, but an honest and rational appraisal of how clothing is used by men to maintain the status quo. With 21st-century eyes, the text can be read as a plea to dismantle patriarchy.

In the paper, Fry gives us a clue as to why this was so difficult then, and why it proves to be so difficult today. He makes reference to Teufelsdröckh, a fictional philosopher created by the Scottish writer Thomas Carlyle in the 1833 novel *Sartor Resartus*, which translates as 'The Tailor Retailored'. The full name, Diogenes Teufelsdröckh, translates as 'God-born devil's dung'.

Carlyle was a racist who had great influence on 19th-century British culture: he was described by Ralph Waldo Emerson as 'the undoubted head of English letters'.

Carlyle's *Sartor Resartus* is a satire about an unnamed editor piecing together Teufelsdröckh's philosophical work *Clothes: Their Origin and Influence*. The most ridiculous thing Carlyle could imagine a philosopher ever writing: a philosophy of clothes.

An excerpt from the imagined philosophy, presented to the reader as entertainment: 'Thus in this one pregnant subject of CLOTHES, rightly understood, is included all that men have thought, dreamed, done, and been: the whole External Universe and what it holds is but Clothing; and the essence of all Science lies in the PHILOSOPHY OF CLOTHES.'

Carlyle wrote *Sartor Resartus* around the time of the Reform Act in England and Wales, which allowed men of certain income or standing to vote.

Carlyle is usually depicted as a thundering old man, dishevelled, as if his thoughts were way more important than the semiotics of his clothes, a vanity trick recently played by a 21st-century British Prime Minister, Boris Johnson.

But this drawing, in the archive of the National Portrait Gallery, reveals Carlyle as a dapper, fashionable, spritely younger man. Look at the jaunt of that leg, one foot wrapped around the other. The drawing is undated. The caption at the top reads: 'Carlyle at British Museum'.

Carlyle ridiculed those who took an interest in clothing while fully embracing its power messaging.

Let's go back to the Apostles for a moment. They were obsessed with style. Their garments were unchanging because of university traditions. Their style obsession manifested itself in how they wrote, how they thought.

In January 1903, Leonard Woolf presented the paper 'What is Style?' He was 23. 'I think it is safe to say that there is a certain element in writing which the majority of mankind are agreed to call style,' he wrote. He is talking about literary style, but the statement can also be applied to style in clothing.

Woolf attempted to give a definition. 'For the style is due as much to the imagination which is expressed by the meaning of the words as to that expressed by the rhythm of the sentence.' Again, it echoes style for clothing: not just what is worn, but *how* it is worn.

He admitted that, initially, he thought there was little practical reason to discuss style, that 'one knew more or less what other people meant when they used the word'. The same is often said of clothes: why bother studying them? But then he realized, 'to fix the meaning of a word like this,' that is, a word like 'style', 'is of practical value for criticism. For there is practically no good criticism because of the vagueness of meaning attached to the technical words which the critic uses.'

I believe this is true of clothes, and their semiotics, within which style plays its part. If we can start to understand clothes, we can start to critique the repressive structures which the language of garments helps to maintain.

How does it feel to live such a life of repression? Our next protagonist will give us some insight, which, for me, is close to home.

E. M. Forster

I had a black-and-white TV in my bedroom when I was a kid. I must have been given it when I was around 11. My parents encouraged me to watch films like *Orphée* by Jean Cocteau, or *Jubilee* by Derek Jarman, shown late night on British TV. I'd watch newer films too, broadcast after hours. It was an easy way to see naked men.

In 1985, the production company Merchant Ivory released *A Room with a View*, based on E. M. Forster's 1908 novel. The book is seen as a lighter, lesser work compared with *Howard's End* or *A Passage to India*. But the film, its clothes, and the removal of those clothes, is deeply embedded in the memory of many queer men my age. I would stay awake late, tweaking the dial and pointing the aerial to get the clearest image possible, for its couple of minutes' glimpse of male flesh.

Three years after *A Room with a View* was published, Roger Fry painted Forster's portrait. A suit, shirt and tie cover Forster entirely, except for his face, a stark, long hand and wrist.

Forster was 32 at the time. It would be another five years before he lost his virginity.

In 1925, E. M. Forster wrote the essay 'Me, Them and You' about an exhibition of work by the artist John Singer Sargent. This is the opening paragraph:

'I have a suit of clothes. It does not fit, but is of stylish cut. I can go anywhere in it and I have been to see the Sargent at the Royal Academy. Underneath the suit was a shirt, beneath the shirt was a vest, and beneath the vest was Me. Me was not exposed much to the public gaze; two hands and a face showed that here was a human being; the rest was swathed in cotton or wool.'

Forster then went on to critique Sargent and his world. Of one portrait, Forster wrote, 'how impossible to imagine that Lord Curzon continues beneath his clothes.'

If only Forster knew of Sargent's secret paintings of male nudes, where the clothes are flung open and discarded, naked men posing, stretched out after bathing, or wrestling. The paintings were never exhibited when Sargent was alive.

At that time, Forster had told only his closest friends of *Maurice*, his own secret work, a novel about imagined queer love. Forster had never been with a man when he wrote it. *Maurice* was not published till after his death.

In his diaries, Forster had long expressed his desire for what lay beneath male clothes. On 22 June 1906, aged 27, he wrote, 'In a steamer with Sheppard from Kew. Depressed: but saw naked bodies – rare & glorious sight: one bargee' – he means someone working on a barge – 'brown & supple, drying himself on heap of ashes, the other sunlit as he leapt into a dark warehouse.'

A few days later, he wrote, 'Reasons against suicide: i. selfish. ii. nature ceaselessly beautiful.'

On New Year's Eve in 1907, the day before his birthday, he wrote, '. . . there's no doubt that I do not resemble other people, and even they notice it.'

That queer body crying out, hidden in plain sight by clothing he longed to shed, so he could reveal the body he yearned to share. So much of his life was lived not able to share it.

Forster is that rare entity: a Bloomsbury figure who did not have sex with anyone else in the group. Forster was beloved by Bloomsbury. Forster would eventually live in

Bloomsbury, taking a flat on Brunswick Square in 1925. When Vanessa Bell painted *Memoir Club*, her record of Bloomsbury's ongoing weekly meetings, we see mostly men, trapped in their tailoring. Forster's long limbs are front and centre, suited.

Forster only wore suits. He didn't care about fashion. So why should we care about his clothes?

This is exactly the thinking I want to disrupt: the idea that only the clothes of someone engaged with fashion are interesting to us. If a human wears clothes, those clothes are interesting. Our concern should not be to judge or rate someone's clothes, but to see what their clothes can say, what is there for us to learn, if we are willing to look.

Rather than ignoring it, we should focus on Forster's clothing: it could tell us much about repressed queer lives in the first half of the 20th century.

It soon became clear. Forster could also help me come to terms with my own repressed queer life, as a young man in the second half of the 20th century.

Edward Morgan Forster kept a photo album. This is his first photo of himself, aged seven months, in 1879. Forster is dressed in a dress.

In 19th-century England, kids' clothes crossed genders, as did colours: there was no pink equals girl/blue equals boy. Forster's father was an architect. He died when Forster was a year old. Forster would live with his mother for the next sixty-five years. Here is Forster as a young boy, with his mother.

Forster is dressed in a velvet suit with lace trimmings. He told his friend and biographer P. N. Furbank that he was 'one of the very last children to be tormented in this manner'.

In later life, Forster recalled investigating his penis at the age of four. He wrote about it in a brief memoir, *Sex*, started in midlife and added to across the years, unpublished in his lifetime. 'I knew this was "wrong" and told my mother who must have said "Dirty" for "help me get rid of this dirty trick" presently figured in my prayer,' he wrote.

The word dirty, with its damning sense of total shame, took hold. 'For years I thought my "dirty" was unique and a punishment: yet looked for the "dirties" of others in *Smith's Classical Dictionary*, and was annoyed when they were concealed by drapery in the illustrations to Kingsley's *Heroes*.' Right from his earliest memories, Forster was tormented by what clothing covered.

The following portrait of Forster as a boy is undated. In his photo album, Forster just captioned it, 'self'.

Forster remembered first desiring men at age 11, in 1890. Five years earlier, the Criminal Law Amendment Act had made any male homosexual act or gesture illegal, punishable by a minimum of ten years in prison. An affectionate letter between two men was enough to warrant prosecution. Only 29 years before, sodomy was punishable by the death penalty.

At the back of this photo, Forster stands next to his mother, behind friends at his childhood home in Stevenage, just north of London. His mother is facing right, looking unamused. Forster is around 14 years old.

The straw boater, the shirt and necktie appear to be what Forster is supposed to wear, rather than what he would choose to wear. He smirks at the camera, his facial expression running against this world of imposition. It suggests a queer interior life, a close scrutiny of the heteronormative world. He wears its garments as dutiful infiltrator, as a way to survive.

Ninety-odd years later, at around that same age, I first saw the film adaptation of *Maurice*, late at night, on my black-and-white TV. I was just like Forster, a dutiful boy at school. So much had changed, and yet so much hadn't.

I knew I was queer around the age of seven or eight. I

remember telling myself, you don't have to think about girls until you're older, until you have to marry. I kept myself to myself, first at a local primary school, then when I moved to a public school. I was ten. By that age, I knew my queerness would be lifelong, and would likely be lonely.

I was a day pupil, but most were boarders. It was a mixed and liberal school, in a town with a train station, so it was easy to escape. I had a survival strategy. I was true to my soft self, but I sublimated my sexuality, presenting to the outer world as inert, unthreatening.

For me, this was self-protection: I knew that if I were to speak or act on my obvious queerness, I would be bullied. I would have faced psychological and possibly physical violence, no matter how innocuous it may have seemed to the bully. It's like there was an unspoken pact: if I kept quiet, I was given a pass. Crucially for me, I had no interest in the approval of those who would have bullied me. I was happy to keep out of their way.

I was dutiful because I knew full well of the queer world outside of school's perimeters, one where I did not have to live life in deference to heteronormativity. I knew about it through magazines, music, fashion and film. One of those films was *Maurice*. It was released when I was 13.

I was dutiful because I knew what came after school was so much more important. But being a dutiful boy inside a human body, with all its yearnings, can be a psychologically dangerous trap. It damaged me, being forced to hide, emotionally unable to neither develop nor practise that intuitive dance: the expression of desire.

In August, I was talking with the young designer Steven Stokey-Daley. We were in the communal area outside his tiny basement studio in Hackney, east London. It was around a month before his spring/summer 23 show, and he also had to finish production on pieces due to be delivered to stores. He hoped he wouldn't have to work all night.

Stokey-Daley is working class, from Liverpool. Here's a portrait of him from school, one he's since cut and spliced.

Stokey-Daley uses fashion to interrogate and subvert the British class system. A couple of months earlier, he'd won the LVMH Prize, seen as the most prestigious award for young designers worldwide, with a cash sum of €300,000. The judges included designers Stella McCartney, Kim Jones, Nicolas Ghesquière; the award was presented by actor Cate Blanchett.

Stokey-Daley had only graduated from the BA Fashion course at the University of Westminster two years earlier.

Back then, I was a visiting lecturer at the college, regularly meeting with the students for one-on-one conversations as they put their final collections together. I took this photo of his work at the degree show. It was inspired by Forster novels, the film *Another Country* and the TV adaptation of *Brideshead Revisited*.

At the college, each student had a pinboard in front of their desks, where they could gather research for their collections. Stokey-Daley's was covered in images from *Maurice*, and a mind-map charting his thoughts about Forster. His dissertation was about homosexuality within public school culture and vintage references in contemporary fashion.

It was in those college conversations with Stokey-Daley that I encountered the idea of homosociality, a theory developed by American academic Eve Kosofsky Sedgwick. It posits 'a continuum between homosocial and homosexual,' as Sedgwick puts it – that is, the potential for queerness in purportedly 'straight' male social relationships. Stokey-Daley's application of the theory: boys at English public schools, such as Eton, form quasi-queer bonds which, when they enter business or government, evolve into a patriarchal web of favours and power preservation.

'It felt like there were six buses just driving towards me and they hit me at the same time,' said Stokey-Daley. The Westminster University campus overlooks Harrow School, one of the most elite public schools in Britain. It has educated seven Prime Ministers, including Sir Winston Churchill. A website selling uniform for Harrow lists its required items, including a straw boater hat and a tailcoat.

Walking past the school and its pupils each day led Stokey-Daley to start researching public schools, sexuality and class. 'I found *Maurice*,' he said. 'It was a huge, massive revelation.' Stokey-Daley had just met his first boyfriend, Leo Meredith, who is also now partner in their label S.S. Daley. 'That's what I mean by a lot of buses hit me at once. I had my first date with Leo two weeks before I started my final year.'

At the time, there had been a spate of anti-LGBT protests at a state school in Birmingham, which made Stokey-Daley think more deeply about his own childhood experiences. He had been educated at a state school in Skelmersdale, just outside Liverpool. 'There was a uniform outside of school,' he said. 'Black North Face jacket, black North Face rain trousers, and 110s.' 110s are a trainer by Nike. To not fit in was to risk homophobic taunts. 'I remember I wore a pair of trousers once, and it was like, "faggot, ohmygod".'

Stokey-Daley described the homosociality of the popular boys, who acted queer but weren't. 'In the changing rooms at school, they all just wanted to see each other naked so badly,' he said. 'If one of their friends was to be homosocial in a playful way, that'd be fine. He identifies with that friend because they both wear the same things. But if it was me, the boy who came to school in trousers and shirt, God forbid, it would have been like . . .' Daley acted horror and disgust.

It echoed my own experience, only I was at a school of heightened privilege. As a queer kid, I found homosocial boys terrifying. They were doing what I wanted to be doing, but they were doing it for social position, hierarchical power. Stokey-Daley has claimed ownership of the homosocial world's look. 'That's my point,' said Stokey-Daley, 'to take that upper-class public-school culture and appropriate it for myself.'

Being within that homosocial public-school world can set you back. I was isolated and alone. I dived deep into counterculture. I concentrated on becoming a journalist. I found an outlet for expression through fashion, but I sublimated my emotional life. I was terrified of HIV/AIDS. I was 27 when I finally found my way to connecting with another man, to having sex.

I understand Forster, and what trapped him in those tailored clothes.

Forster gained a place at King's College, Cambridge in 1897. There is only one known photograph of him there, echoing the journey of the Stephen sisters: an abundance of family photographs, but an absence of imagery in the first years of independence. Forster is seen reading in his lodgings, during his final year of study.

Dutiful tailored jacket, hi-rise with a small lapel of no flamboyancy, pocket square, shirt, slacks, barely any of himself showing. Forster became an Apostle in 1901. He was Apostle number 237. It was through the Apostles that Forster came under the influence of G. E. Moore, and became friends with Leonard Woolf, Lytton Strachey and

John Maynard Keynes. He was part of a secret male society, but this brought him no closer to expressing or acting on his desires and feelings.

Forster with his mother, a year after graduation, at their family home in Putney, south-west London. Although his mother is the one with the corseted waist, Forster wears clothes that, for him, are just as confining.

A photograph of Forster, same year, same spot. He wears a hat, a cape, and the faint rumblings of a smirk.

Forster's career as a fiction writer was brief, with four of the five novels he published in his lifetime appearing between 1905 and 1910. His use of clothing in his fiction reveals his frustration and sadness at the heteronormative confines within which he found himself.

A short work, *The Story of a Panic*, was the first he ever wrote. It features a 14-year-old, upper middle-class 'indescribably repellent' boy on holiday in Italy, forming a desperate bond with a local waiter, 'with his arms and legs sticking out of the nice little English-speaking waiter's dress suit, and a dirty fisherman's cap'.

Later that night, the boy is rescued by the waiter, who was 'attired in a dress coat, without either waistcoat, shirt or vest, and a ragged pair of what had been trousers, cut short above the knees for purposes of wading.' The working-class waiter, with flesh exposed, is the only character capable of care in the whole story, his clothes stripped of their decorum.

In Forster's first novel *Where Angels Fear to Tread*, lead male character Philip Herriton 'was a tall, weakly built young man, whose clothes had to be judiciously padded on the shoulder in order to make him pass muster.'

Judicious padding is a trick of bespoke tailoring, building a scaffold on the supposedly inadequate body to present a strong-shouldered, and therefore masculine and powerful, silhouette.

And then there was *A Room with a View*. One hour and one minute into the film adaptation, there are three minutes and fifteen seconds of full-frontal male nudity.

Actors Rupert Graves, Julian Sands and Simon Callow play characters who mess around naked in and around a secluded pond.

We see them shed their clothes. In the novel, Forster describes the men's actions around the pond, not their bodies. There is no lusting needed in his words – their nakedness is enough. But Forster gives their piles of shed clothes an active role in the scene. The clothes have a voice.

And all the time, three little bundles lay discreetly on the sward, proclaiming:
'No. We are what matters. Without us shall no enterprise begin. To us shall all flesh turn in the end.'

Forster gives these clothes a voice of admonishment and control. It is not human bodies that act, it is the persona created by the clothing worn. Clothes have expressive power.

The naked men attempt an insurrection against their clothes. They kick the bundles, throw the garments. Forster described the action, as well as what he desired in his own queer life, with five words:

Clothes flew in all directions.

At the time, Forster was hopelessly in love with a young student, Syed Ross Masood. Masood was handsome, six feet tall. Masood was straight. It was an unrequited love that would last for years. Here is Masood with Forster, their clothes very much not flying in all directions. Masood is so buttoned up that not even the flesh of his neck can be seen.

In his diary on 31 December 1909, Forster wrote, 'You've stopped me. I can only think of you, and not write. I love you Syed Ross Masood: love.'

That year, Forster first met Virginia Woolf, at a Thursday evening gathering hosted by Lady Ottoline Morrell. In 1910, his Bloomsbury group status was confirmed when he was invited to read a paper to their Friday Club. It was titled 'The Feminine Note in Literature', a version of which he'd read to the Apostles earlier in the year. Woolf was much taken by his words. Forster wrote in his diary, 'Miss Stephen said the paper was the best there had been, which pleases me.'

Forster was already friends with Leonard Woolf through the Apostles. After the Woolfs married, Forster would visit them. This photo of Forster with Woolf is undated, but Forster is young, and in his diary on 6 July 1913 he wrote, 'Typical of my feebleness that I have put off writing my diary because the ink doesn't match and have not described my weekend at Woolf's, who with Virginia and Strachey were nice to me.'

That body, hidden in clothes, still untouched. He was 34.

A couple of weeks later, he wrote about his body. 'The life of the flesh is best,' reads the entry for 26 July 1913, 'but it's better to subdue the flesh than to let it become subterranean.'

His body obsessed him. He went on to consider his hair, 'my companion for over thirty years,' he wrote. 'I understand why hairs are used in magic. And nothing so prefigures the final diffusion of the body. They symbolise death.'

Visible hairs on the body are made up of dead cells. Forster is saying that we walk around every day on this bridge between living and dead. He continued, 'I have rejoined the universe, and don't expect to be more conscious of the union when I have joined it entirely.'

Here is Forster with his hairs, his body trapped in tailoring, aged 36, such a stark difference to the bodily liberation being lived by Duncan Grant.

Forster was a conscientious objector. In 1915, he headed to Alexandria, Egypt, to serve as a Chief Searcher with the Red Cross, looking for missing servicemen.

While there, he observed young, carefree and naked men, but unlike the remove he felt when observing nude men from a steamer in 1906, his words had softened. It felt closer to something he too could experience.

He wrote that 'hundreds of young men are at play,' and that they' go about bare chested and bare legged, the blue of their linen shorts and the pale mauve of their shirts accenting the brown splendour of their bodies; and down by the sea many of them spend half their days naked and unrebuked . . . It is so beautiful that I cannot believe it has not been planned.'

A photograph from Forster's album of men swimming naked in the sea at Alexandria. It's likely Forster took it – I can feel his yearning.

In 1916, Forster had sex for the first time, anonymously, with a soldier on the beach. It left him feeling dissatisfied. In 1917, he struck up conversation with a young tram conductor, Mohammed el Adl. This photograph of el Adl is in Forster's photo album.

On the back, Forster stuck a tram ticket.

The pair tentatively felt their way towards sleeping together. They began a physical relationship. At the age of 38, Forster was finally able to express and explore the desires and instincts of his body.

This photograph of Forster is from 1917, the year he began his relationship with el Adl.

It is the first photograph in Forster's album where he smiles. It is the first photograph in his album where his shirt is unbuttoned. As with Grant, clothing amplifies his release.

In 1918, el Adl told Forster he planned to marry. In July, they visited a tailor, ostensibly to buy a suit for el Adl. It was purposefully made too big for him, so they could both wear it.

Forster returned to England in January 1919, after three years in Egypt. A drawing of Forster from that year by Duncan Grant shows us that, on his return to England, separated from his love, el Adl, he was once again buttoned up, in a tie. Gone was the unbuttoned self-expression of Egypt.

That summer, Virginia Woolf was struck by Forster's demeanour. 'I met Morgan Forster on the platform at Waterloo yesterday; a man physically resembling a blue butterfly – I mean by that to describe his transparency and lightness.'

Woolf went on to describe him further. 'I like Forster very much, though I find him whimsical & vagulous to an extent that frightens me with my own clumsiness & definiteness.' Vagulous means wayward, vague, wavering.

And yet Forster's mood was bleak. Back in Egypt, el Adl had been imprisoned under false firearms charges. Forster wrote in his diary about the prospects of his own dutiful life. 'I am happiest when busy,' he wrote on August 12. 'How fatuous! I see my middle age as clearly as middle age can be seen.'

A year after Woolf's 'blue butterfly' observation, Forster stayed with her at Monk's House. In her diary on 24 April 1920, Woolf made observations about Forster's temperament, that he was 'obstinate about "niceness" – much of a puritan. Tells the truth. I wish I could write his talk down.' She remarked on his questions of style and taste for Leonard: 'Where d'you get your boots? Are Waterman pens the best.'

Woolf also repeated herself: 'Morgan came for a night. Very easy going; as sensitive as a blue butterfly.' To me, that reads as his sublimation of his emotional reality: on the surface, light as a butterfly; beneath, bitter turmoil.

Following is Forster at Monk's House, a man apparently as sensitive as a blue butterfly. He appears weighted by his garments. His tailored jacket is so long and all-encompassing it's like a button-front minidress.

That year, Forster wrote an essay titled 'Notes on the English Character', eventually published in *Atlantic Monthly* in 1926. He was 41.

In the text, Forster describes the typical life passage of middle-class men. He plots their course through the English fee-paying public school system to positions of authority and wealth. These men are headed 'into a world of whose richness and subtlety they have no conception. They go forth into it with well-developed bodies, fairly developed minds, and undeveloped hearts.'

It was the year the British Empire reached its territorial peak, colonizing around a quarter of the planet's land area. 'And it is this undeveloped heart that is largely responsible for the difficulties of Englishmen abroad,' Forster wrote.

That word, 'difficulties', understates the centuries of murder, enslavement, rape, abuse and theft committed by Englishmen abroad, as well as the Englishmen at home who controlled, or profited from, Empire and the slave trade.

And yet Forster's intuition about 'undeveloped hearts' echoes the lovelessness that bell hooks would cite as the root of societal malaise in her work *All About Love: New Visions*, published in 2000. 'There can be no love without justice,' wrote hooks, before going on to say: 'abuse and neglect negate love. Care and affirmation, the opposite of abuse and humiliation, are the foundation of love.' She later wrote: 'It is a testimony to the failure of loving practice that abuse is happening in the first place.'

Forster used garments to define his archetypal Englishman and his undeveloped heart: 'the national figure of England is Mr Bull with his top hat, his comfortable clothes, his substantial stomach, and his substantial balance at the bank.'

Male clothing is so entrenched in set ways of patriarchal thinking, it is not questioned. Men wore 'comfortable clothes', as in the articulated suit, its tailored lines helping to hide this 'substantial stomach'.

It's the same in the 21st century. Men in political power wear suits. The suit plays a key role in consolidating and signalling power. It has been the uniform of male authority for so long, we are supposed to just acquiesce to its wearers' claims to power.

'The main point of these notes is that the English character is incomplete,' wrote Forster, before continuing, 'It has a bad surface – self-complacent, unsympathetic, and reserved. There is plenty of emotion further down, but it never gets used. There is plenty of brain power, but it is more often used to confirm prejudices than to dispel them.'

In 1921, Forster spent time in India, serving as secretary to the Maharajah of Dewas. Here is Forster, in what was described as 'his full official robes of an Indian court'.

Forster took pleasure in Indian garments. The dhoti, a style of sarong that resembles baggy trousers, was eroticized for him. He recorded in his diary a three-day trip to Bidar, a city he visited with Masood. 'I have forbidden my imagination to stray beyond the facts into licentiousness,' he wrote on 18 November. 'There it was, two lads . . . knives at the waist, dhoti like a glass cloth.'

Forster, fifth from the left, joins the Maharajah of Dewas, third from the left, in a game of juju.

Forster found the Maharaja to be a lazy, uninterested ruler, in contrast to the conviction, clarity and will of the growing Indian independence movement. This served as the backdrop to *A Passage to India*, Forster's final novel, the last time he would write fiction about heterosexuals and their undeveloped hearts.

In 1924, Forster inherited his aunt's house in Abinger Hammer, Surrey. The village took its name from its water-powered iron forge, which closed in 1787. Forster and his mother moved in. Living with his mother may have cramped his style, but it also provided cover. Forster never married, unlike other queer humans in Bloomsbury who used that heteronormative construct as their veil.

Existence in the village was quiet, constrained. Forster was 45, newly emboldened to approach men he desired. These were not the men of undeveloped hearts in their suits. Forster fancied working men.

His eye was caught by a bus driver who, on first glance, reminded him of el Adl. The driver's name was Reg, or Tom, Palmer. He was married with a child. Forster had this photo of Palmer in his photo album.

Rolled-up shirt sleeves are a symbol of a labouring man, as opposed to the suit-wearer, whose jacket sleeves keep the shirt beneath held to the wrist. The sleeves of Palmer's shirt are rolled up so high, it's unlikely they could go further. How convenient to show off those muscled arms.

Palmer told Forster he'd never had sex with a man before. Forster was in the middle of the protracted move to the house he'd inherited, meaning his old house was often empty, and available. Unbeknownst to his mother, Forster and Palmer would meet there for sex.

It was no way to live. In 1925, Vanessa Bell helped Forster rent a flat in Bloomsbury. He led a double life: in Abinger, chaste; in London, man on the scene. Forster had found a way to use his tailoring to help him get the men he wanted. As he said about his suit in 'Me, Them and You', 'I can go anywhere in it' – his tailoring was his passport within the patriarchal world.

In 1926, Forster became lovers with Harry Daley, a policeman. Daley was 25 and openly gay, using his charms to operate above the law he was supposed to enforce. Daley is said to have inspired *Dixon of Dock Green*, a beloved British police TV series that ran from 1955 for twenty years. Duncan Grant painted this portrait of Daley in 1931.

Grant's portrait fetishizes the uniform. Daley is entirely covered, but to queer eyes the coded language of the garments tells a different story. The portrait speaks of the presumed power and dominance of the man beneath. The suggestion of a belly held by the belt confirms him as an archetypal 'real man'. It speaks of fantasies in which a policeman forces a suspect to submit, or conversely, a suspect gets the upper hand.

Forster was attracted to uniforms and the men who wore them. In 1929, he was travelling through Toulon, the base of the French navy, on the south coast of France. He picked up a sailor, Achille Morgenroth. Forster was 50. A year later, Morgenroth gave Forster this photograph.

On the back, Morgenroth had written, '<u>souvenir</u> à mon ami Morgan'.

The photograph is stamped with the name of a photography studio, Robert, with an address on the quay at Toulon. On eBay, there are similar portraits by Robert of handsome young sailors. The sailors are unnamed, adding to the sense of transience, anonymity and sexiness. The sailor's uniform tells of men who've been away from women for some time. The cleanness of its white striped top and white pants, gives the tension of innocence about to be undone. The sailor's uniform remains a fetishized outfit of desire among gay men.

Another photograph given to Forster by Morgenroth, this time written 'à mon cher ami Morgan' – to my dear friend Morgan. It's dated 1930.

They corresponded for years, the letters from Morgenroth sometimes asking for help with money. In 1934, Forster visited Morgenroth, who had moved back to his hometown of Forbach, right on the German border. They spent the weekend in a hotel, Morgenroth passing Forster off as 'an uncle in the clothes trade,' wrote Forster's biographer P. N. Furbank, 'to account for Forster's dowdy appearance.' His middle-aged drag had some benefits.

Forster's affair with Daley had quickly dwindled because Daley was too comfortable with his sexuality: Forster needed the shadow play of a seemingly straight man who relents. Still, Daley had his uses. He lived in what was called a section house in Hammersmith in West London. It was a boarding house for young male police officers, who lived there until they married. At the time, it was common for a job to offer not just paid work, but also accommodation.

In 1934, Lord Snell raised the issue of London's police section houses in the House of Lords. He said the policemen who lived there were 'healthy, virile, and at an age when they are most susceptible to temptations which need not here be mentioned.'

Snell continued: 'It is sufficient to say that these temptations exist, and that the conditions under which these young men are compelled to live are such as to induce them to seek relief from them in more than one undesirable way.'

Snell was the son of farm workers who became a socialist politician and campaigner. He never married.

It was in the Hammersmith lodgings that Forster met 28-year-old Bob Buckingham. The story was the same as with Reg Palmer: Buckingham said he'd only ever slept with women. The pair felt their way to a physical relationship, and then to deep love. This photograph of Buckingham was taken in 1931.

Forster's photo album shows the quick blossoming of their relationship, and the garments they wore so that their illegal love could exist in plain sight. Here's Buckingham in July 1931, sitting on a park bench in London. He's out of police uniform, in the uniform of heteronormativity.

Forster, on the same bench, in similar heteronormative uniform. Presumably, the lovers took the images of each other.

A month later, they holidayed together in Arles, France.

Theirs was not a monogamous relationship. Forster let Buckingham sleep with women. In 1931, Buckingham started seeing May Hockey. In 1932, Buckingham told Forster that Hockey was pregnant. Single parenting was frowned upon. They would swiftly have to marry.

The night before his wedding, Buckingham spent the night with Forster. At the ceremony, Forster was a witness, one of only five people present. For months afterwards, Forster felt so bereft, he 'pretended I should kill myself'. That year, he wrote in his commonplace book: 'Yes, I wish I could have died. To kill myself – no, frightening, also selfish.'

Forster found a way to exist. Bob and May Buckingham had a son, Robert Morgan Buckingham, the middle name a tribute to Forster. May Buckingham allowed Bob to keep seeing Forster. So began an unspoken understanding, a relationship and friendship that would last the rest of Forster's life. 'I have been happy for two years,' wrote Forster. 'From 51 to 53 I have been happy, and would like to remind others that their turns can come too. It is the only message worth giving.'

The pair travelled widely. In 1935, they stayed in Holland with the writer Christopher Isherwood and his partner, Heinz Neddermeyer. Here is Buckingham, smoking his pipe, with Neddermeyer.

Their polite tailoring belies mortal peril. Isherwood and Neddermeyer had fled Germany in 1933, the year Adolf Hitler declared the Third Reich. Neddermeyer was German, falling in love with Isherwood in the previously liberal society of Berlin. Hitler's Nazis would go on to murder 600,000 homosexuals.

Isherwood and Neddermeyer travelled Europe and North Africa, trying to find sanctuary for Neddermeyer. They failed. In 1937, he was expelled from Luxembourg and forced to return to Germany. Neddermeyer was arrested by the Gestapo, and sentenced to three and a half years forced labour and military service.

In 1938, Forster wrote the philosophical essay 'What I Believe'. It is an affirmation of decency, tolerance and personal relationships, as well as a critique of belief itself. He writes against hero-worship and power. 'I hate the idea of causes, and if I had to choose between betraying my country and betraying my friend, I hope I should have the guts to betray my country.'

Forster ends the essay wishing to shed garments and the role they play in enforcing hierarchy, power. 'Naked I came into the world, naked I shall go out of it!' he writes. 'And a very good thing too, for it reminds me that I am naked under my shirt, whatever its colour.'

Someone was paying attention. In 1943, the artist Paul Cadmus wrote to Forster from his home in New York. Cadmus expressed his admiration for 'What I Believe' and included photographs of works inspired by Forster's words. The following work is titled *To E.M. Forster*.

Cadmus was a painter. He was also part of the queer photography collective PaJaMa, with his lover Jared French and Jared's wife, Margaret Hoening. In 1937, they had combined the first two letters of their first names, and begun photographing each other, often naked, mostly on the empty wide-horizon beaches of Fire Island or Provincetown, both queer havens. PaJaMa embraced self-expression, open love, creativity: this was a collective that echoed the Bloomsbury group.

Forster and Cadmus corresponded often. In April 1947, Forster crossed the Atlantic for the first time to spend three months in the US. He burst in on Cadmus and French in their New York apartment. 'The flat is Bloomsbury and insanitary,' he wrote, finding connection with a way of living where creativity came first.

Forster travelled across the States and returned to New York in June, staying at their place. Cadmus and French were already in Provincetown, with Cadmus's lover George Tooker, and Forster headed out to visit them. Here are Forster, Tooker and Cadmus: a generational shift revealed in their clothing. Tailoring for Forster, rolled-up shirt sleeves for Tooker and Cadmus. Forster was 68.

Before Forster travelled to Provincetown, he spent the night in New York with Jose Martinez, a young dancer. The pair cruised the Rambles in Central Park, an area where men met for anonymous sex.

Forster had this photo of Martinez in his album.

And this one.

Forster in the June heat of Provincetown, still wearing his suit, in which he can go anywhere. Look! That smile.

Forster had this photo of Paul Cadmus on the Provincetown sand dunes in his album. Cadmus wrote on the back that they 'sat below this dune the day we took that walk with you'. That's Cadmus, in the foreground.

Cadmus had begun work on a painting titled *What I Believe*, which he finished in 1948.

The painting sets art and creativity against the horror of war, taking Forster's 1938 essay as inspiration. There, overseeing all, on the centre left of the work, is Forster himself. That's him, looking to his right, his arms outstretched, palms facing up.

Finally, Forster had shed his clothes. He was seen.

Forster lived long, 91 years. In 1963, he wrote the following in his unpublished memoir, *Sex*.

Adding when I am nearly 85 how annoyed I am with Society for wasting my time by making homosexuality illegal. The subterfuges, the self-consciousness that might have been avoided.

Listen to his anger. As I write, 59 years later, there are 69 countries in the world where homosexuality is illegal. In 10 countries, homosexuality is punishable by death.

In the UK today, it's easier for a lanky, soft, awkward queer human such as Forster to find a place for themselves. I am one. I was born in 1973, three years after Forster died. I remember the pain I felt as a young kid, of imagining my future life unrealized. It felt tight, like the bitter tightness in Forster's words. It felt like my life was likely to be wasted.

I'm writing this in the British Library. I'm wearing a sheer black caftan and a tiny pair of shorts. It's easy to consider this a victory of progress, freedom and liberation.

In his essay 'What I Believe', Forster spoke against the Christian church and 'Faith with a large F', stating that its influence in modern society 'is due to the money behind it, rather than to its spiritual appeal'.

In the United States, the Supreme Court recently overturned Roe vs Wade, eliminating the constitutional right to an abortion. Judge Clarence Thomas said the court should also reconsider rulings on same-sex marriage, and even same-sex intimacy.

Since then, multiple anti-LGBTQ+ laws have been introduced in the USA, including laws banning gender affirming care for transgender youth, laws aimed at restricting drag performance, and laws that censor school curricula. In the United Kingdom, transgender people find themselves increasingly demonized and used as pawns in political games. This is the reality of our apparently progressive world.

We've seen how clothes were a veil for Forster. Next, we'll spend a moment considering how clothing provided cover for others in Bloomsbury, whether for politics, forbidden desire or gender.

Two Stracheys and Carrington, or, The veil of clothing

Let's head back to Studland Beach. On holiday with the Bells in 1910 were the couple Desmond and Molly MacCarthy, and Marjorie Strachey, Lytton's sister. Clive Bell has his back to us. That's Marjorie Strachey lying between the MacCarthys. She is holding up an edition of the suffragette newspaper *Votes For Women*. We can see by her eyes that she's smiling.

She's in a sweater, a long skirt. There's no sign of any restrictive undergarments. The look is chic. Suffragettes wore smart garments to infiltrate polite society, to cause change from the inside, rather than dressing to stand out.

Marjorie Strachey was a suffragist and vocal activist for women's rights, rare within Bloomsbury circles. Most didn't get involved.

Similarly smart is the tailoring of her brother, Lytton. Strachey's clothing echoes his manner, seeking dominance and control. He was gossip puppet-master of Bloomsbury, taking pleasure in creating bad blood. 'What scandals! What disclosures!' he once wrote of his own correspondence.

Here he is, standing outside the Gower Street home of Lady Ottoline Morrell, a supposed friend about whom he had been relentlessly cruel. He's wearing his puppet-master uniform: double-breasted tailoring.

Earlier in life, Strachey had been lover of both Grant and Maynard Keynes. This is Strachey aged 38, dressed in more casual clothes, but still portraying masculine dominance, his hand on the head of Dadie Rylands. Rylands would go on to become a noted theatre director. The control of Strachey's stance! Ryland's trousers are hitched so high they're almost empire line.

Later in life, Strachey had a relationship with the publisher Roger Senhouse.

Senhouse was 19 years Strachey's junior, and was happy to get naked. As with fellow Bloomsbury males Forster and Keynes, Strachey does not reveal himself.

Their relationship was sadomasochist. Senhouse was the provider of the pain. In this next photo, that's Senhouse to the left, wielding the stick. Strachey wears his masochist's uniform of double-breasted tailoring: those in power may secretly want to be punished.

In July 1930, Senhouse staged a mock crucifixion of Strachey, cutting him on his side. A year later, Strachey died, aged 51, from undiagnosed stomach cancer.

The artist Carrington is usually viewed through the prism of Lytton Strachey. It's clear why: Carrington was devoted to him, taking her own life two months after Strachey died.

This is Carrington. The photo is undated. That patterned sweater is as glorious and deliberate a choice as her cropped hair. Today, many are inspired by her style.

Carrington self-identified by her surname alone, dropping her first name, Dora, after arriving at the Slade College of Art in 1910. She was known as Carrington throughout her life, yet, since her death in 1932, her self-identification has not been respected – today, the website of the Tate misnames her.

Carrington was 17 when she began studying at the Slade, the first wave of young adults to benefit from the actions of

Bell and Woolf's generation, their rejection of restrictive dress. Here's Carrington, on the left, with friends Barbara Hiles Bagenal and Brett. Together they were known as the Cropheads, their haircuts abrupt, outside the Slade in 1911.

In 1915, Carrington wrote to the artist Mark Gertler, who was obsessed with her. He would not take no for an answer. 'You must know,' she wrote, 'one could not do what you ask, sexual intercourse, unless one does love a man's body. I have never felt any desire for that in my life'.

This sounds so familiar. It's like that letter Woolf sent to Leonard Woolf, the one where she felt no more than a rock. Here again we have a queer woman trying to make herself heard. And yet Carrington is still considered in relation to men.

Carrington did sleep with men, such as Ralph Partridge, whom she married in 1921. For a while, Partridge was also sleeping with Lytton Strachey. Here's Partridge, proudly wearing his buff rower's body.

'You know I have always hated being a woman,' Carrington wrote to writer Gerald Brenan in 1925. They'd had a relationship, but Carrington was now trying to explain to him why it was over: 'I am continually depressed by my effeminacy.' She told Brenan that she could derive pleasure from penetrative sex, but that 'afterwards a sort of rage fills me because of that very pleasure.'

The year before, she'd had an affair with Henrietta Bingham. 'Really I had more ecstasy with her and no feelings of shame afterwards.' She continued that she had 'a day-dream character of not being female'. If Carrington were alive today, she'd be able to explore non-binary as a way of finding peace with her gender. As it is, history's view of her is stuck in a binary.

Maybe we should consider her expressive clothing not just as fashion inspiration. Here is a human, in the face of patriarchy, using clothes to try and tell us who they are.

We'll meet with Carrington again, soon.

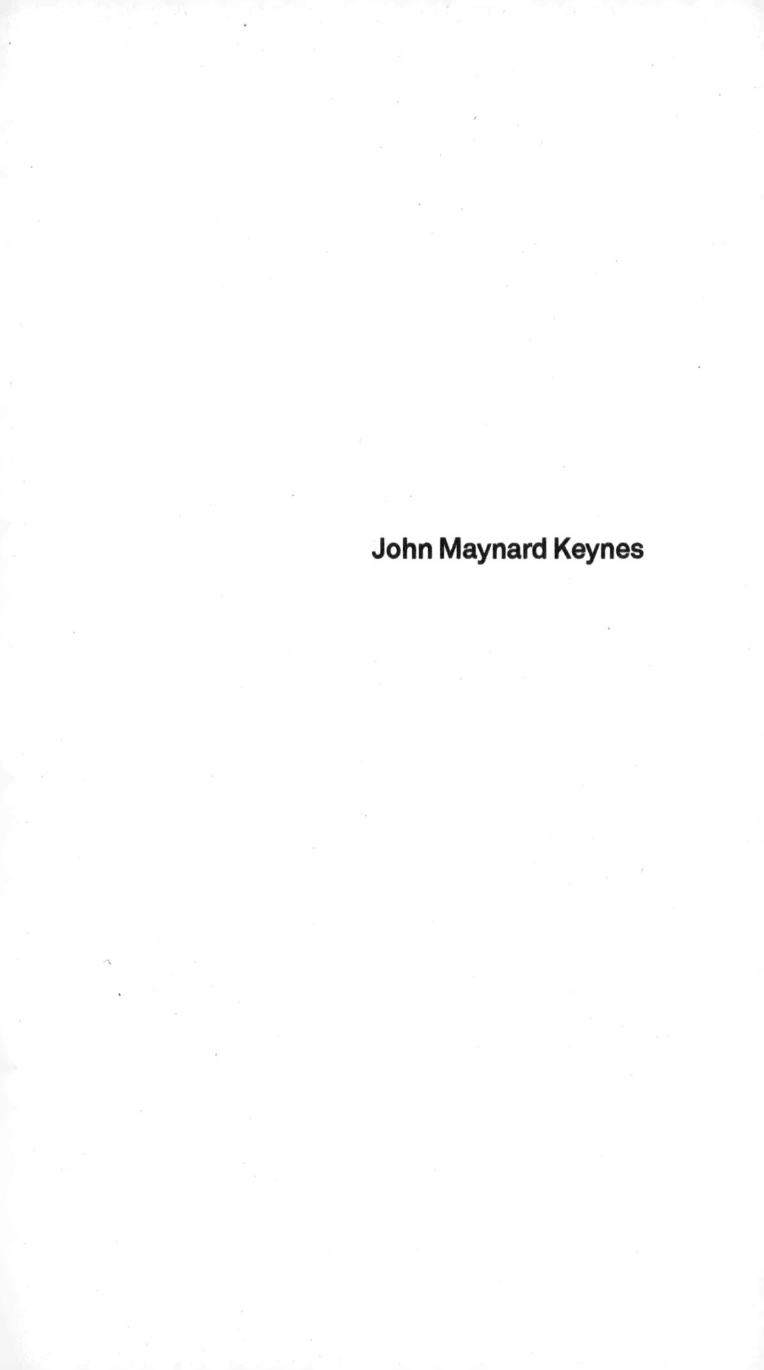

John Maynard Keynes

When John Maynard Keynes was born, his father, John Neville Keynes, wrote in his diary, 'They say that the boy is the image of me. It's ugly enough.' The next day, he wrote, 'I am already getting very fond of him, notwithstanding his ugliness . . .'

An immediate paternal legacy of lovelessness. Aged 17, Keynes wrote to Arthur Hobhouse, a fellow student at Cambridge University, who would become his lover. 'I have a clever head, a weak character, an affectionate disposition, and a repulsive appearance.'

A year later, he sent this to Lytton Strachey, another soon-to-be lover: 'My dear, I have always suffered and suppose always will from a most unalterable obsession that I am so physically repulsive that I've no business to hurl my body on anybody else's.' He continued that 'the idea is so fixed and constant' that he didn't think anything 'could ever shake it.'

Yet at Cambridge, Keynes developed a philosophy of beauty that should have shaken it. 'Appearance is in fact relative to him who looks,' he wrote in his 1905 paper 'A Theory of Beauty'. He meant that there was no universal idea of handsomeness or repulsiveness. 'There is no such thing,' he continued, 'as objective appearance.'

Keynes would spend his life wearing the mask of suit, shirt, tie, plagued by self-loathing. He was part of the post-World War I generation who consolidated the suit as the garment of power and wealth.

I have often been repelled by tailoring, even though my focus as a fashion critic has been on menswear. What is it about the suit that embodies what I do not want to be, have never wanted to be? What is it that has led me to spend a critical life often in opposition to it? Keynes, and his life of lovelessness, offers some insight.

One-year-old Keynes in a ruched velvet dress with lace collar, a jewelled bow on the waistband – garments similar to those worn by Forster as a young child.

Keynes two years later, in another belted and ruched dress. Across his lap he is holding a shotgun.

Aged 14, Keynes went to Eton College. The following photograph is captioned 'Fags serving tea to their fagmasters'. That's Keynes, a fag, standing tall at the very back.

Fagging was a system at English public schools where older boys – the fagmasters – took on responsibility for the well-being of those younger than them – the fags. In return, the fags would perform menial tasks for the fagmasters, such as polishing their shoes, cooking them breakfast or serving their tea. Corporal punishment – caning – was the norm. It was preparation for a life of lovelessness: tasks and acts of generosity performed as duties, rather than out of a sense of community or compassion, never reciprocal.

This is the homosocial world at its most hard-boiled. Look back at how garments codified the fags and fagmasters: dutiful tailoring for the fags, their elaborate dress showing that these submissive humans were still of the upper classes. Because he was already tall, Keynes went straight into wearing a black morning suit with tails, black silk top hat and white bow tie, rather than the spread collar and black tie of his smaller peers. For the fagmasters, the gregarious stripes of their sporting blazers show that these former fags had now earned their pleasures.

Eton taught its students about the power and uses of a shared patriarchal uniform. Keynes's biographer Robert Skidelsky quotes an old Etonian as saying: 'you could think and love what you liked: only in external matters, in clothes, or in deportment, need you do as the others do.'

Keynes enjoyed his time at Eton, particularly because he was sleeping with his friend Alfred Dillwyn 'Dilly' Knox, the son of a bishop. According to a detailed list of men he'd slept with, the first initials, in 1901, are A.D.K.:

PP/20A/2

1901 A.D.K.

1902 A.D.K.
D.M.

1903 Nil.

1904 Nil.

1905 Nil.

1906 G.L.S.
J.B.S.
A.L.H.

1907 G.L.S.
J.B.S.

1908 G.L.S.
J.B.S.
D.G.

1909 J.B.S.
D.G.
St G.
Stable boy of Park Lane

1910 D.G.
F.B.
St G.

1911 D.G.
Jack Colly
Rosario Sciacca
Sixteen year old under Etna
Auburn haired of Marble Arch
St G.
Lift boy of Vauxhall
Blackman. boy 13

1912 D.G.
G.K.S.
Jackey
Chester 16

1913 D.G.
St G.
Chester
F.B.
Corkie
Brush
Salem
Cairo 22
B.K.S.

1914 St G.
B.K.S.
Corkie
Delkin
D.G.

1915 D.G.
B.G.
F.B.
G.L.S.
Grip
Tresidder
Corkie 26

Here's Keynes at Eton, sitting on the right, acting in *The Rivals* by Richard Brinsley Sheridan. Keynes was in his final year.

In 1902, Keynes headed to Cambridge to study mathematics. It was here he first met future Bloomsbury friends. Not long into his first year, he was picked out by Lytton Strachey and Leonard Woolf as an Embryo for the Apostles. On 28 January 1903, he became Apostle number 243.

It was the year that G. E. Moore would publish *Principia Ethica*. Later in life, Keynes looked back on this formative time in his paper 'My Early Beliefs', read out to Bloomsbury's regular meeting, the Memoir Club, in 1938. He said that Moore's book, 'and the talk which preceded it and followed it, dominated, and perhaps still dominate, everything else.'

Moore opened the door to consideration of what was good. 'The appropriate subjects of passionate contemplation and communion were a beloved person, beauty and truth,' he said in 'My Early Beliefs', 'and one's prime objects in life were love, the creation and enjoyment of aesthetic experience and the pursuit of knowledge.' Next came a key line. 'Of these love came a long way first.'

Keynes's prime object in life was love, yet he found himself part of a loveless society. From 1903 to 1905 at Cambridge, Keynes was a 'higher sodomite': engaged in idealist discussion about same-sex love without actually doing it. From what I remember of my Philosophy studies, this was a common trait in the classic texts: men writing endlessly around a subject without saying what they wanted, within a codified white male world, making overarching statements about how humans are, without paying attention to those who were not given equal opportunities in life.

Keynes came to know Duncan Grant through Lytton Strachey. Keynes and Strachey were sleeping together; Grant was Strachey's cousin, and Grant and Strachey had been lovers. In late June 1908, Keynes and Grant fell in love.

It was a hopeless situation, the pair attempting an illegal relationship while living in two different cities: Keynes in Cambridge, Grant in London. Keynes was needy. Between 10 July and 15 August 1908, he wrote 23 letters to Grant. Often, he sent one each day.

Grant replied 14 times. On 6 August, he wrote to Keynes, 'I am no letter writer.' Grant had an untethered spirit. We can tell from Keynes's words that Grant left him hanging. 'I feel that I want you very much this evening, and I can't expect even a letter for several days,' Keynes wrote on 28 July. Next day: 'This is no letter at all. I only send it because you may like to see my hand-writing on an envelope. Dear

Duncan, I never come into my room without a vague hope of seeing yours. JMK'

A letter from Grant arrived on 31 July, but by 4 August, after writing daily letters back, Keynes was getting desperate. 'Dearest Duncan, I am getting in the most miserable condition. For some reason or other, depression has descended, and of course it has fixed itself on you, so that I think about you more than I should and even lie awake to do it and suggestions that I shall never see you again won't be kept out of my head.'

A reply from Grant arrived the next day. However much these letters were longed for, they could also be dangerous. 'I have to take the greatest care here,' wrote Keynes on 8 August, 'for the housekeeper who looks after one's clothes is she who wrote anonymous letters to la B a year or so ago charging Scott with nameless things – so your letters never leave my person through all changes of clothes.' The clothes that masked their love could also jeopardize it.

It sounds so intense: the constant carrying round of letters, the threat of imprisonment if their relationship was revealed. Today, the threat in the UK is gone, but there is still something of an echo. It's not so different from the iPhone that's in my pocket right now, all the secrets it carries, always with me.

That year, Grant painted a portrait of Keynes. Grant would later say, 'Maynard with his writing board was a good subject, so while he was immersed in the "Theory of Probability" I . . . was immersed in trying to figure out the shape of his face.' From this, Keynes began to appreciate the work of artists, and that 'he accepted, without me having to point it out, that the painter had a serious job at hand.'

The tailoring looks soft, comfortable. The shined shoes are fancy. There is intimacy in his forward lean, the ballet-like point of the foot. Keynes wrote to Grant to say his family had been to see the painting. He said their 'general attitude' was of 'surprising approval', but they wondered 'why my trousers aren't turned up'.

Keynes's garments had meaning to Grant. He also painted a portrait of Keynes without Keynes, by painting a portrait of his hat, shoes and pipe. I wish I could show you the painting – one image of it exists online. The work is somewhere in a private collection, as yet unfound at time of publication.

As we have already seen, they were now more buddies than boyfriends. Keynes's letters remained as constant and voluminous as before, but were less clingy. In March, Keynes was holidaying with friends in Devon, spending his time playing golf. His eyes were roaming, he was happy to tell Grant about it.

'I play badly but am much consoled by the most charming caddie in the world, whom I've chartered,' he wrote. A golf caddie carries a golfer's bag. 'We spend every afternoon tramping round the links together, and I'm falling deeply in love. He really is lovely – gaiters, coat and jersey, naked neck and Devonshire voice. He despises me rather, but is extraordinarily kind . . . And I shall never be able to kiss him. What a bloody world!'

Consolidated here was a shadow world of gay patriarchy. Those in the middle and upper classes were dressed and able to do as they pleased. Along the way, they fetishized those subservient to them, the men and their clothes, like the caddy, whose name Keynes either doesn't know or doesn't think worth sharing.

This gay patriarchy was often misogynist. Keynes had started lecturing on economics in 1909, as well as coaching individual students. 'I think I shall have to give up teaching females after this year,' he wrote to Grant in February 1909. 'The nervous irritation caused by two hours' contact with them is <u>intense</u>. I seem to hate every movement of their minds. The minds of the men, even when they themselves are stupid and ugly, never appear to me so repellent.'

Keynes was embracing the power of the suit and all it

stood for, fetishizing it and playing with it. This next photograph was in an album from his 1910 holiday with Grant. It is of an unspecified male. Maybe to some eyes the pose is innocuous, but to queer eyes, the subject is showing off their butt.

The tension in the tailored cloth, particularly the pulled-apart fabric, is heightened by the pose: facing the wall, submissive.

I first saw the photo in the Archive Centre at King's College, Cambridge. One research trip, it clicked: wasn't that arch in the courtyard outside? The archivist, Patricia McGuire, and I headed out. The photo wasn't taken on holiday at all. It was taken directly below Keynes's rooms at the college, which he'd moved into only the year before, and which would remain his for the rest of his life. Being given these permanent rooms was a mark of his standing at the college.

The same spot, 102 years later, now with added parking sign, and blinds at the window.

When we know its location, beneath his bedroom window, the photograph of the submissive suited man, presumably taken by Keynes, assumes even greater connotations of sex, possession and control. Who was Keynes sleeping with in 1910? His list, which we saw on p.213, details three:

D.G.
F.B.
St G

The figure is not D.G. – Duncan Grant: the hair is too straight, the body is too fleshy: Grant was lithe his whole life. St G was a 17-year-old dancer called Francis St George Nelson. The body in the photo is not that of a 17-year-old dancer. My guess: the photo is of Francis Birrell, whom Keynes would call Frankie, son of the Chief Secretary to Ireland. If it is Birrell, the suit shows his place in the establishment, this submissive pose his subversion of it.

As Keynes's academic reputation grew, so did his pleasure in codified clothing. Keynes wrote to Grant on 28 October 1910, saying that his company was 'becoming more fashionable than formerly, but incredibly unintellectual', and that 'I care no longer for anyone who doesn't wear elaborate clothes and play at least one game rather well. I think it's chiefly their clothes, I like.'

Maybe his tongue was in his cheek, but he also sounds tickled at that evening's prospects. 'In an hour I'm going to a dinner party (for the first time in my life) drawn from such circles,' and went on to list their names: a fashionable golfer; someone who was 'more loose than his more famous brother'. 'We sit in dress clothes: our menus have our names stamped on in gilt. What on earth am I doing there?'

A letter to Grant the next month gives a clue. He tells of Cecil, unknown surname, who was drunk after a dinner, bursting into Mr Collin's room 'in evening dress and very good looks, immensely garrulous and lascivious, showering kisses on us (rather nice ones) and muttering in my ear that he wanted to copulate with everyone but particularly with Gerald.' Gerald is likely Gerald Shove, a fellow Apostle.

Keynes loved sex. He shared with friends his statistics, written in a code that has still not been cracked: what do 'c', 'a' and 'w' stand for? Those stats:

AP/20A/1

		c	a	w	total	
1906	May13 - Aug12	4	11	4	19	
	Aug - Nov	1	8	7	16	
	Nov - Feb	3	12	4	19	
1907	Feb - May	3	12	4	19	= 73
	May - Aug	2	20	3	25	= 79
	Aug - Nov	1	15	3	19	= 82
	Nov - Feb	2	18	1	21	= 84
1908	Feb - May	1	12	3	16	= 81
	May - Aug	17	4	4	25	= 81
	Aug - Nov	28	0	3	31	= 93
	Nov - Feb	16	4	2	22	= 94
1909	Feb - May	20	4	2	26	= 104
	May - Aug	12	7	2	21	= 100
	Aug13 - Nov12	13	4	0	17	= 86
1909	Nov - Feb	16	3	2	21	= 85
1910	Feb - May12	10	3	3	16	= 75
	May13 - Aug12	1	9	5	15	= 69
	Aug13 - Nov12	8	6	6	20	= 72
	Nov13 - Feb12	7	9	2	18	= 69
1911	Feb13 - May12	11	5	2	18	= 71
	May13 - Aug12	16	4	5	25	= 81
	Aug13 - Nov12	3	8	2	13	= 74
	Nov13 - Feb12	9	2	1	12	= 68
1912	Feb13 - May12	6	6	4	16	= 66
	May13 - Aug12	12	4	0	16	= 57
	Aug13 - Nov12	4	10	5	19	= 63
	Nov13 - Feb12	8	6	4	18	= 69
1913	Feb13 - May12	7	7	4	18	= 71
	May13 - Aug12	11	6	3	20	= 75
	Aug13 - Nov12	7	8	4	19	= 75
	Nov13 - Feb12	4	7	2	13	= 70
1914	Feb13 - May12	10	3	1	14	= 66
	May13 - Aug12	8	5	0	13	= 59
	Aug13 - Nov12	7	6	0	13	= 53
	Nov13 - Feb12	7	5	1	13	= 53
1915	Feb13 - May12	7	7	5	21	= 60
	May13 - Aug12	7	6	5	18	= 65

James Strachey once described Keynes as 'the iron copulating-machine'. In 1911, Keynes sent Strachey a brief letter that ended, 'I hope you will find the enclosed useful.' With the letter was a small brochure for L. Raymond Surgical Rubber & Book Store, which promised on its cover 'Waterproof sheeting, enemas, Douche cans . . .'

I found the brochure Keynes sent Strachey among his letters in the British Library. Most of its pages inside are taken up with listings for 'French and Spanish Skins' and 'American Rubber Tips', i.e. condoms. The cover of the brochure reassures discretion for any enquirers: 'Mr RAYMOND opens all Correspondence himself, and destroys them same day.'

Consumerism for Keynes wasn't clothes shops, it was sex shops.

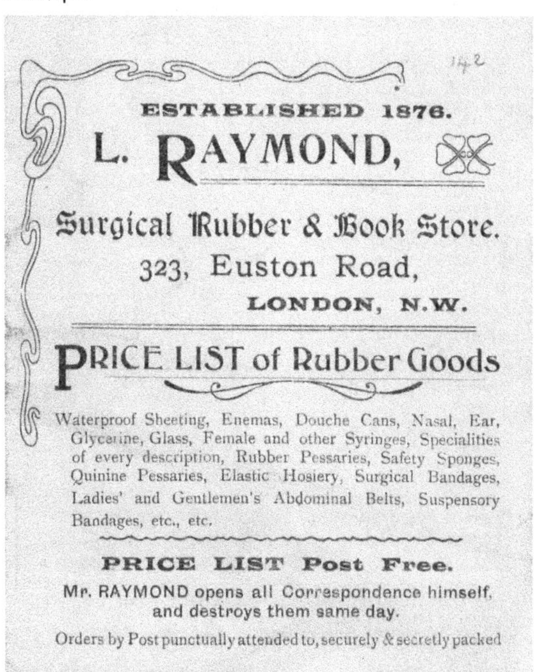

Look at the body language in this photo of Grant and Keynes.

It was taken in 1912, at Asheham, the country home of Virginia and Leonard Woolf. Both are entirely masked by their tailoring. Grant holds his hands in front of him, as if to say, no fun today. Keynes's pose says, let's have some fun.

Keynes has his hand shoved hard into his left pocket, pushing his crotch outwards. It's like that photo from behind of the suit jacket spread over a butt. Keynes's pose breaks with the respectfulness of the tailored suit. It says, I want more now. It also says, I claim power.

At the outbreak of World War I, Keynes was called in to the Treasury to help with a monetary crisis. Sudden, unexpected conflict had caused a breakdown of the structures for international payments. By January 1915, Keynes had been given a job within the Treasury itself.

Despite the war, social life continued. Lady Ottoline Morrell took this photograph of philosopher Bertrand Russell with Keynes and Lytton Strachey at her country home, Garsington. Morrell was having an affair with Russell. 'Keynes,' wrote Russell to Morrell that year, 'was hard, intellectual, insincere, using his intellect to hide the torments in his soul.'

In her image, Morrell is having fun with three humans unified by their tailoring and their hats, knowing that each of them, beneath their tailoring, is of distinct individual character.

Keynes's friendship with Duncan Grant endured. He was also fond of Vanessa Bell, and of Charleston, Bell and

Grant's home. Keynes had his own room, contributing to the rent. He would spend many weekends there, still dressed in his tailoring.

Grant painted his portrait in the garden at Charleston. Keynes is said to be drafting a telegram to negotiate a loan from America to ensure the economic survival of the United Kingdom. Keynes is wearing a bi-coloured hat at odds with his grey tailoring. It is noticeable that Grant paints Keynes, the man who thought himself repulsive, as particularly handsome.

The painting depicts Keynes dedicated to his work, but he may not have been as resolute as the image suggests. In a letter to Grant later that year, Keynes wrote, 'I work for a government I despise for ends I think comical.'

Indeed, the mood of Grant's portrait was not as intimate as it may appear. Roger Fry was also present, painting Keynes from another angle. Fry's portrayal of Keynes's face, as well as the line of his stomach, shows that Grant's portrait was the artist's equivalent of Facetune.

It was common for Keynes to be dressed in tailoring when in pastoral settings. This next photo, from his own album, was taken in 1918. The braces confirm that the trousers are from a time when they were tailored to sit at 'true waist', the crotch usually covered by the skirt of the jacket. Over the 20th century, functional styles, such as chinos and jeans, would lower the waistband of trousers, which now usually sit just above the hips. If necessary, they are held in place by a belt – the pull of braces would hoist contemporary trousers too high.

I was looking through a box of photos of Charleston, and thought, there's a copy of that Grant and Keynes photo from 1912 – the one with Keynes's hand thrust in his pocket. Then I noticed: Keynes has a bald spot here, but didn't in the other one. I checked: the photo from 1912 is against a brick wall, this one is in front of a closed wooden gate. It was a different photo.

Their pose is near identical, but the second photo was taken six years later, three years after Keynes stopped recording his sex partners. This time, Keynes has his hands on his hips, spreading the front of his jacket to keep attention on his crotch. As in the other photo, his right leg is suggestively forward. Grant was still lowering the portcullis with his body-language, Keynes still punting for a chance.

After the German surrender of 1918, Keynes became part of the British Delegation at the Paris Peace Conference. The Prime Minister, David Lloyd George, had just won a snap general election. His victory was secured by seeking reparations from Germany, regardless of Germany's ability to meet such demands.

Keynes spent the first half of 1919 working on the peace treaty, but became increasingly disturbed by the talks. He felt these were stuck on punishing Germany rather than rebuilding Europe. He resigned from the Treasury in June. 'Dear Prime Minister,' he wrote on 5 June 1919, 'I ought to let you know that on Saturday I am slipping away from the scene of nightmare. I can do no more good here.'

Keynes retreated to Charleston to write about his experiences. Here he is at Charleston in 1919, that familiar hand-thrust-in-pocket pose.

The resulting book, *The Economic Consequences of the Peace*, became an immediate global bestseller. In it, he spelt out both the impossibility of Germany paying its reparations, and the avarice of the victors' demands: 'nations are not authorized,' he wrote, 'by religion or by natural morals, to visit on the children of their enemies the misdoing of parents or of rulers.' Many have seen the book as prophetic of the rise of Nazism, and World War II.

The Economic Consequences of the Peace is mostly comprised of financial calculations and arguments. But, in a celebrated passage, Keynes describes the clothing of French Prime Minister Georges Clemenceau, one of the Council of Four, alongside Prime Minister David Lloyd George of Great Britain, Prime Minister Vittorio Emanuele Orlando of Italy and President Woodrow Wilson of the United States of America.

'The figure and bearing of Clemenceau are universally familiar,' wrote Keynes. 'At the Council of Four he wore a square-tailed coat of very good, thick black broadcloth, and on his hands, which were never uncovered, grey suéde gloves; his boots were of thick black leather, very good, but of a country style, and sometimes fastened in front, curiously, by a buckle instead of laces.'

Keynes lingers with delight over these details, particularly the gloved hand. Later he wrote that Clemenceau 'carried no papers and no portfolio', and that he 'spoke seldom, leaving the initial statement of the French case to his ministers or officials; he closed his eyes often and sat back in his chair with an impassive face of parchment, his grey gloved hands clasped in front of him.'

Keynes knew what he was doing, focusing on those gloved hands. They sent such a damning message of imperviousness, superciliousness. Keynes described a recurring cycle of endless meetings with the Council of Four, the impassioned Lloyd George and Wilson 'all sound and fury signifying nothing', while Clemenceau sat 'silent and aloof on the outskirts', 'throned, in his grey gloves, on the brocade chair, dry in soul and empty of hope, very old and tired, but surveying the scene with a cynical and almost impish air'.

During the negotiations, Keynes became friends with Dr Carl Melchior, a banker who was negotiating for the Germans. Keynes wrote about Melchior in a talk for the Memoir Club, which he gave in February 1920. Melchior's clothing is used as an indicator of intelligence, patience and decency. Keynes said that the Germans at the talks were a 'sad lot', with 'drawn dejected faces and tired staring eyes'. Then came Melchior.

'But from amongst them stepped forward into the middle place a very small man, exquisitely clean, very well and neatly dressed, with a high stiff collar which seemed cleaner and whiter than an ordinary collar'.

With Melchior, Keynes worked to try and ensure food supplies were delivered to a destitute Germany.

Here is Melchior on the left, and Keynes on the right, by a train in Trèves, France, in 1919. On that train, Keynes had first met Melchior, during financial discussions between the British, Americans, French, Italians and Germans. In the middle is Dudley Ward, who had been part of the Neo-Pagans, a Bloomsbury-aligned group centred around the poet Rupert Brooke.

Keynes and Melchior remained friends. Melchior was Jewish. In 1933, he was dismissed by the Nazis from his role as board member for the Bank of International Settlements. He had already suffered from heart problems, and died, that December, from a stroke.

On Thursday 26 May 1921, Virginia Woolf wrote in her diary about a conversation she'd had with Keynes in a Bloomsbury square. Keynes was 38.

I sat in Gordon Square yesterday for an hour & a half talking to Maynard. Sometimes I wish I put down what people say instead of describing them. The difficulty is that they say so little. Maynard said he liked praise; & always wanted to boast. He said that many men marry in order to have a wife to boast to.

It's such a brief passage in Woolf's diary, yet these words shouted off the page at me. Keynes's words give crucial insight into a fundamental pivot in his life. Neither of the two main biographies of Keynes mentions this conversation. The motivation behind his words struck a chord with me.

Towards the end of 2016, when I was 43, I remember thinking: I want to live differently. I was single. I'd had a few years of super-fun casual sex, finally understanding in my late 30s and early 40s how to get what I wanted. But I faced a toll of emotional emptiness.

I wanted to be nourished by love. I actively decided to open myself up to the possibility of finding love, which I may have previously pushed away, or not recognized, or thought I had found but had been mistaken. A few months later, in March 2017, I met my now husband, Rich.

Keynes's conversation with Woolf sounds like a similar self-declaration. He, like me, had recognized a need for something more. Yet his options were severely limited by society, since he could not openly be in a relationship with a man, let alone a marriage.

Six months later, Keynes went to the opening night of *The Sleeping Princess* at the Royal Opera House in London. Its star ballerina was Lydia Lopokova. Three years before, Keynes had written to Grant about Lopokova, describing her dancing as 'poor'. To another friend, a stockbroker named Oswald 'Foxy' Falk, he said of her, 'She's a rotten dancer – she has such a stiff bottom.'

But Keynes went to see this production of *The Sleeping Princess* over and over, sitting alone in the stalls. The pair began a relationship. For the first few years at least, Keynes continued to see men, notably Sebastian Sprott, 14 years his junior and an Apostle. That's Sprott on the right, at Charleston in 1921 with Douglas Davidson, an artist who was sleeping with Duncan Grant.

Keynes with Lopokova, on holiday in Dorset in either 1922 or 1923.

Keynes was now a public figure with a global platform. Here he is, keeping up appearances in his tailoring, at the Genoa Conference of 1922. It was an attempt by 34 nations, led by British Prime Minister David Lloyd George, to rebuild defeated Germany and to forge links with Soviet Russia. Germany and Russia ignored the conference and signed their own treaty. It was at the Genoa Conference that the return to the gold standard was first mooted.

Here's Keynes, over-accessorized with hat, cane and watch chain across his stomach. Note that his trousers are, by now, turned up: his parents would have been pleased.

In his world of public display, a heteronormative society where male homosexuality was illegal, Keynes could only form a flourishing, enmeshed, unhindered relationship with a woman. This was a relationship that could be in the open, one in which Keynes could boast, and receive praise: the blessed banality of everyday love.

Still, at the time, there were some men who, usually protected by class privilege, were living in open and flourishing same-sex relationships. Edward Carpenter was an English poet and campaigner for socialism and gay rights. Carpenter was friends with E. M. Forster, who wished he could be more like him. 'Forward rather than back,' Forster wrote in his diary on 31 December 1913. 'Edward Carpenter! Edward Carpenter! Edward Carpenter!'

For thirty years, from 1898, Carpenter lived openly with his partner, George Merrill. Carpenter's example shows what it took to be able to form a same-sex relationship, one where you could boast and seek praise. You had to be a radical. You had to take a stand.

But Keynes was part of the establishment. 'Keynes was no socialist,' wrote Paul Krugman, economist and columnist for *The New York Times*, in 2007. 'He came to save capitalism, not to bury it.' Today we'd likely describe Keynes as centre-left, which really means centre-vaguely-right. He evolved radical thinking about the economy, but it was within capitalist confines.

When Keynes said to Woolf that 'men marry in order to have a wife to boast to', it sounds like he meant: queer men, trapped within convention, who cannot form unhindered relationships with each other, marry women in order 'to have a wife to boast to'.

I found it heavy going, being in Keynes's world. During the days of reading his letters, written in his hand, I would feel depressed. All those words, never really saying what he wanted to say. After one such day of research, I sat at a dinner next to the artist Rita Keegan. It had been the hottest day ever recorded in the United Kingdom, the temperature reaching 40.3°C. We were eating outside, in

Vauxhall, just south of the river Thames. A sharp storm was forecast but scant few globs of rain brought relief.

Keegan was wearing a sleeveless top she had made herself, sewn from printed fabric. She had studied fashion in the sixties in her birthplace of New York, before heading to San Francisco and switching to art. She moved to London in 1980. Keegan was talking about clothes and their history. 'Cotton is slavery,' she said.

Something clicked. In Keynes's *The Economic Consequences of the Peace*, he set out a brief history of British and European economics in the late 19th century. He stated that investment abroad 'enabled the Old World to stake out a claim in the natural wealth and virgin potentialities of the New.' He continued that 'the whole of the European races tended to benefit alike from the development of new resources whether they pursued their culture at home or adventured it abroad.'

To accept Keynes's theories is to accept, and not question, this claim.

The language of power embodied in the modern tailored suit was cemented in this time. To wear a suit today is to carry this inheritance: tailoring signifies acceptance, not questioning, of the colonialist claim.

In the 1920s, Keynes spent time trying to help the ailing cotton industry in Lancashire. For *Nation & Athenaeum* magazine, he wrote that 'Lancashire has found, since the war, a worsened competitive position and diminished markets for her American cotton goods.' The industry imported bales of cotton from the United States. The effects of war were still being felt, compounded by Churchill's ill-advised restoration of the gold standard.

Keynes tried to help the industry, but it was no use. The old system was collapsing, following more than 250 years of horror. Britain had enslaved and exported millions of humans. After slavery was abolished in 1833, British industry continued to rely on cotton that had been picked and cleaned by enslaved people. After the United States abolished slavery in 1865, cotton pickers still lived and worked in inhumane conditions, suffering from racism and exploitation.

Keynes was blinkered to the reality of the cotton industry, as he was to the reality of capitalism and empire. He was not alone – it was the mindset across the United Kingdom. It continues. Today, the production of cotton yarn is rife with exploitation and injustice. If you are wearing cotton now, you are highly likely to be complicit in it, even if that cotton is labelled with words like 'organic'.

Some may excuse Keynes by saying, that's just how people were back then. But even if we use these blinkers, his work is still in jeopardy. His theories are based on economic models that harnessed enslavement, empire, exploitation. As we shall see, his emerging personal beliefs reinforced the problem.

Keynes and Lopokova married in 1925 at St Pancras Register Office. There were six guests, including Duncan Grant as a witness. A quiet wedding, yet it was a hot media story. Outside was a throng of journalists and photographers, outnumbering the wedding party by over a hundred. We see mostly a sea of suits, with just that one man, and those two children, looking at the camera as if to say, what is going on?

An undated photograph of Keynes with what looks like his wife, found in the boxes at Charleston. It is unclear why the photograph is burnt.

The pair were well matched. Keynes's photos give us a glimpse of their private downtime camp, which involved play with appearance. Mr and Mrs Keynes, at home in Tilton, their residence not far from Charleston.

Keynes in the garden with a lampshade on his head. He was free, frivolous, and fully suited.

Keynes strikes a pose with a group of unidentified men.

Another visitor was Sir John T. Sheppard, a former lover of Keynes, who had become provost of King's College, Cambridge.

Mrs Keynes, at home, wearing what's described as an 'African mask'.

It was 1927. In Keynes's papers is the pamphlet for the first World Population Conference, held in Geneva for four days beginning 31August. Keynes was listed as being on its Advisory Council. Members of its General Council included Dr E. Baur, likely to be German geneticist Erwin Baur, and Dr Eugen Fischer. Their work on human heredity from 1921–32 was a key influence on Adolf Hitler's *Mein Kampf.*

Baur died in 1933, the same year that Fischer signed a pledge of allegiance to Hitler. His work provided 'evidence' for the racist and anti-Semitic Nuremberg Laws in 1935, and between 1937 and 1938 he examined over 600 Afro-German children, who were then sterilized. Fischer became a member of the Nazi Party in 1940, and, as director of the then Kaiser Wilhelm Institute of Anthropology, Human

Heredity and Eugenics, he worked on using physiological specifications to determine racial origins. He died in 1967.

Keynes was chairman of the Malthusian League, named after the 18th/19th-century economist Thomas Malthus, who believed that population growth would outstrip food production, causing degradation of wealth unless population was reduced by war, famine or disease. His theories are often cited by those who believe in population control.

This had been part of Keynes's worldview for some time. On 2 May 1914, he opened a discussion at the Political Philosophy and Science Club in Oxford, titled *Is the problem of Population a pressing and important one now?* 'Almost any measures seem to me to be justified in order to protect our standard of life from injury at the hand of more prolific races,' he wrote in his paper for the discussion. 'Some definite parceling out of the world may well become necessary; and I suppose that this may not improbably provoke racial wars. At any rate such wars will be about a substantial issue.'

In 1927, Keynes gave a speech to the Malthusian League, in which he stated, 'I believe that for the future the problem of population will emerge in the much greater problem of Heredity and Eugenics. Quality must become the preoccupation.'

Eugenics is a belief in selective breeding in humans; it is often tightly coupled with racism.

Keynes, on holiday, gripping his wife. They are joined by two unidentified men. The unidentified man on their right is wearing plus-fours, a fashion in sporting garments, with roomy pants that finish four inches below the knee. The unidentified man on their left cuts a sharp line, from the curve of his back over his butt to his ankle. Acceptable menswear styles, yet ones of recognizable flair.

Keynes in his tailoring in 1932. On his left is John T. Sheppard. On his right is an unidentified young man.

Jaunty Keynes, in soft tailoring and flat cap. He was 49.

In 1937, Keynes became vice-president of the British Eugenics Society. His name appears on the inside front cover of that year's Annual Report, listed with five other vice-presidents. This listing of his name implies that he agreed with its contents. Page two is titled 'THE AIMS AND OBJECTS OF THE EUGENICS SOCIETY'.

It states that it 'seeks to awaken a eugenic or racial conscience'. Under a bold heading '**Race Mixture**' it states:

In certain circumstances, race mixture is known to be bad. Further knowledge of its biological effects is needed in order to make it possible to frame a practical eugenic policy. Meanwhile, since the process of race mixture cannot be preserved, great caution is advocated.

Under a bold heading '**Immigration**' it states:

In view of the possible effects on the national stock of admitting persons of varying quality, the biological aspects of the regulations governing immigration, and the plans for emigration within the Empire should be regarded as a matter of urgent study.

It argues for voluntary sterilization, segregation, marriage for 'defectives' only after voluntary sterilization, health examinations before marriage.

The report goes on to detail its current research. It states the awarding of a fellowship 'to investigate the literature of race mixture'. It continues that the subject 'is of biological importance in many parts of the British Empire and in one European country has become a political issue'. It does not name the country, but that country is likely to be Nazi Germany.

A professional portrait of Keynes, from around that time.

A year earlier, Keynes had published *A General Theory of Employment, Interest and Money*, which has been interpreted as a plea for government spending and intervention, as opposed to free markets. These are so-called 'Keynesian beliefs'. Reading it again, I was struck by this passage at the end. 'For my own part,' he wrote, 'I believe that there is social and psychological justification for significant inequalities of incomes and wealth, but not for such large disparities as exist to-day.'

He thinks there should be some inequality, just not this much inequality. Why?

He states that 'dangerous human proclivities can be canalised into comparatively harmless channels by the existence of opportunities for money making and private wealth, which, if they cannot be satisfied in this way, may find their outlet in cruelty, the reckless pursuit of personal power and authority, and other forms of self-aggrandisement.' Really?

He continued. 'It is better that a man should tyrannise over his bank balance than over his fellow-citizens; and whilst the former is sometimes denounced as being but a means to the latter, sometimes at least it is an alternative.'

Notice that Keynes genders this, suggesting methods for men to channel their lovelessness. It made me think back to that quote from a contemporary of Keynes at Eton: 'you could think and love what you liked: only in external matters, in clothes, or in deportment, need you do as the others do'. Tailoring and money go hand-in-hand, allowing men to treat others as playthings.

It was on 9 September 1938 that Keynes read his paper 'My Early Beliefs' to the Memoir Club, who had gathered at his home in Tilton. 'I remain,' he said at one point, 'and always will remain, an immoralist.' He went on to recall the Apostles of Cambridge: 'We were among the last of the Utopians,' who could 'be safely released from the outward restraints of convention and traditional standards and inflexible rules of conduct, and left, from now onwards, to their own sensible devices, pure motives and reliable intuitions of the good.'

This is the ivory tower of the Apostles and, to a certain extent, of Bloomsbury. The devotion to what was good blinkered them from what was real.

Keynes sitting in his tailoring, mid-Atlantic, in 1946, to his right a naval officer.

That year, Keynes represented the Eugenics Society when it awarded its first Galton Gold Medal, named after its founder, Francis Galton. Keynes said Galton was a 'genius', and that 'Galton's eccentric, sceptical, observing, flashing, cavalry-leader type of mind led him to become the founder of the most important, significant and, I would add, *genuine* branch of sociology which exists, namely eugenics.'

The British Eugenics Society eventually changed its name in 1989 to the Galton Institute. In 2019, its then president, Veronica van Heyningen, stated that Galton was 'a terrible racist'. Sixty-six days after he called the terrible racist Galton a genius, Keynes died of a heart attack. He was 62.

What the Bloomsbury servants wore

In 1922, 18-year-old Grace Germany wrote a brief memoir of her life so far. 'My name in full,' she began, 'Grace Jeannette Germany, daughter of George & Elizabeth Germany, born in the year 1903, in the month November, on the 4th day, in the village of Banham.' Banham is a village in Norfolk, in the east of England.

Germany left school in 1917, aged 14. In the UK, the school-leaving age would not rise to 16 until 1972. She went to live with her aunt and uncle in Hayes, then in the county of Middlesex, but now part of Greater London. 'Worked in stamp, jam, & Gramophone Factories.' Gramophone records had recently become the main format for at-home music listening, what we would today call vinyl. On 20 December 1917, she was back, summoned home by her father: her mother was seriously ill with pneumonia and expected to die. 'Went home, mother got better,' she wrote.

She begged her parents to let her go into domestic service 'but giving no reason', she said. She first worked for Doctor Sourant in Norwich. 'Was very unhappy as the Doctor had an awful temper so left on May the Eighth, 1920.'

Without work, she applied for housemaid placements at Collins Agency in Norwich: 'from there got Mrs Bells address and came to London on 30th June 1920'.

She would be employed by Vanessa Bell and Duncan Grant for the rest of her working life.

A portrait of Grace Germany, aged 17.

On April 28, she wrote, 'boredom is increasing not decreasing.' I'll quote her next day's entry at length: the Quentin she refers to is Bell's second son.

I do not wonder that people commit suicide, or even murder. Life sometimes grows so monotonous, there is no wish to live. I sometimes think, 'I wonder if it would hurt if I killed myself', then another time, I am terrified at the sight of a knife or a needle in Quentin's hands, as he is so fond of pretending to push it into me. I wonder if it is how some crimes are commited, the same thing every day, nothing to change the monotony, until one feels one must do something or go mad, then someone comes in while one is in this mood, and in desperation you crack that someone over the head with

something. The mood passes & you come into your proper senses to see the awful thing that is done.
Then comes the discovery by the police, the trial & found guilty by the jury.
Then Death.
All because the monotony of Life.

It is stark: the rage, frustration, self-hatred she had to accept and sublimate. Germany would marry, become Grace Higgens, and go on to be described by Duncan Grant as the 'Angel of Charleston'. Bell painted her portrait in the kitchen of Charleston. It now hangs upstairs at the end of the corridor, next to Grant's door. It shows us the typical uniform of domestic servants.

The primary functional purposes of the uniform are both practical and psychological. Sleeves are pushed back for the hard labour of cooking, cleaning, washing, stoking and tending to the fires that heated the house. The white apron protects her garments beneath, dealing with and revealing the inevitable and constant dirt. The uniform demarcates Higgens as a servant, denied the same privileges and rights as the other humans at Charleston.

When we talk about the philosophy of the Bloomsbury group, we must accept the reality that underpinned their philosophy of living. Domestic servants were central to the homes and lives of Virginia and Leonard Woolf; Vanessa Bell and Duncan Grant; John Maynard Keynes; Lady Ottoline Morrell. They lived life in pursuit of the good, but it was only 'the good' for certain people.

Outside of work, the garments of Higgens and her colleagues reveal an easier take on functionality. Here is Higgens in a light, simple, sleeveless summer dress.

It would be no surprise if it were handmade. The photograph was loose in her archive papers. Other photos had been stuck in a book, with captions by Higgens. Here's a spread of two such photos.

They wear garments of elevated functionality, decorating the body yet allowing ease of movement. These dresses feel so familiar today. I'm writing this in the dog days of summer. London's heat still in the high 20s, after months of barely any rain. This morning, a hosepipe ban came into force in the capital, to try and mitigate the drought.

Dresses like these, in light, comfortable cloth and of roomy cut, have become prevalent. I have friends who wear them daily. I know directors of companies, owners of restaurants, editors, who live their lives in such dresses.

Functional clothing is usually taken to mean pieces like the chore jacket, which has crossed over from worker's garment to fashion item. As we can see from the photographs of Higgens and her colleagues, these dresses have followed the same path from labourer to fashion. This is reappropriated functionality.

Higgens knew she looked good: check her caption on the right.

I love the shape of the dress worn by Alice, on the right.

Woolf's domestic servants had a similar relationship with their garments. This is Annie, presumably Annie Chart, and

Lily, whose surname I can't source. They were picking apples, though it looks more like they are posing as if they were picking apples.

On the following page, another tree, different looks. A functional dress for the unidentified domestic servant on the left, a patterned and pocketed long apron for the domestic servant on the right.

Today, manufactured versions of these garments could be sold for hundreds of pounds. Those that construct such garments could do so for little pay. Those who deliver such garments to online customers could likely be on zero hour contracts, working maximum hours for minimum wages with few rights. Inequalities are rife.

The clothes of these workers make me want to get back to the sewing machine. I need to learn how to make pockets.

Lady Ottoline Morrell

October. I was inspecting a dress once worn by Lady Ottoline Morrell, a patron, friend and frenemy of the Bloomsbury group. It was in the research rooms at the Fashion Museum in Bath, which holds Morrell's collection of dresses and fabrics. Acid-free tissue paper lined the table to protect the clothes; white gloves were on our hands. A pile of garment boxes was to one side, holding the collection. We had a lot to get through.

The dress is long sleeved, cut from velvet, long through the body, its bottom section fishtailing out. There is no corsetry to restrict flesh. It has exaggerated shoulders, a puffed-up style that could be called leg of mutton, held by a band of black velvet across the biceps. There is lace trim and beading at a squared neck and cuff.

Morrell stood six feet tall. I am no photographer. No matter how far back I went, it was hard to get all of the dress in one image.

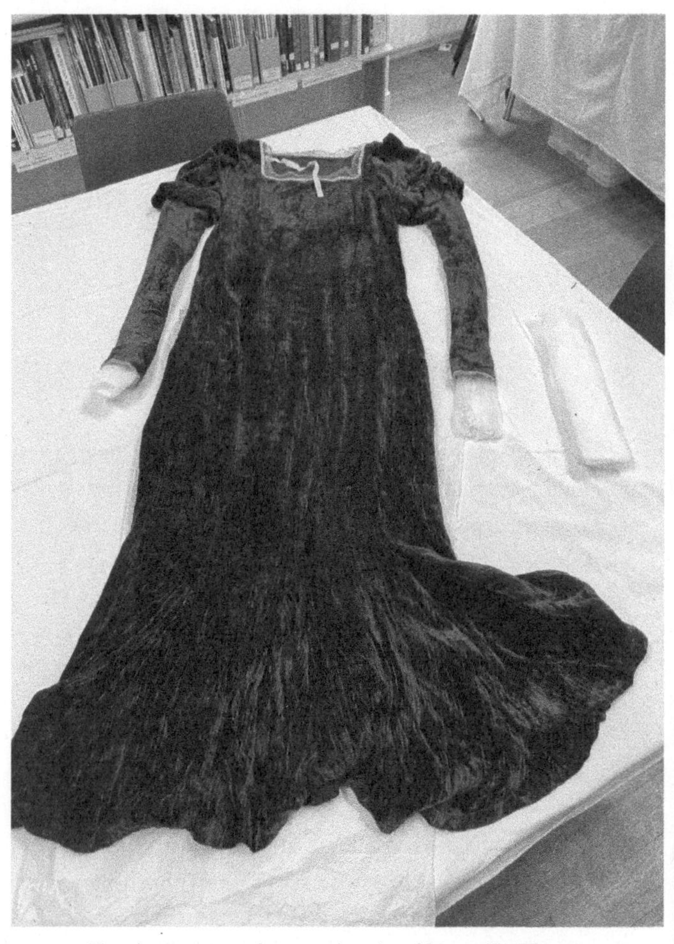

The dress was a favoured style of Morrell's. There were four near-identical versions for me to look over. Eleanor Summers, the Collections Manager at the Fashion Museum, pointed to the finish of the lace neckline and suggested it was handmade.

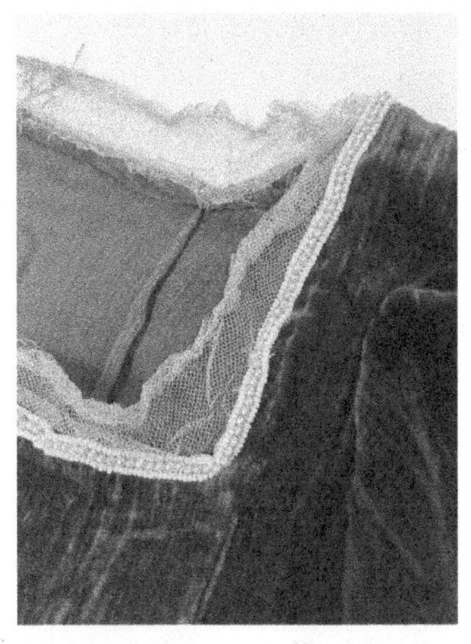

But wait, what was that? There was a hole in the fabric. Summers said it was likely a cigarette burn.

I was selecting pieces for the exhibition at Charleston. The Ottoline Morrell collection had never been exhibited before. In the end, out of these four near-identical velvet dresses, we chose to display the one with the least food down the front.

Here it was. After all this absence, finally, an actual wardrobe of clothes worn by a member of the Bloomsbury group. It was glorious. Morrell's hats had been laid out for me to see.

These pieces were wildly familiar. In 1919, the artist Augustus John, a former lover of Morrell's, painted her portrait. He had done many others of Morrell, but this work is now one of his best-known.

It is likely the clothes she wore in the portrait were in the room with us. When Morrell first saw John's painting, she wrote in her journal, 'the top part of the face is fine and tragic like me, but the mouth is too open and infinite – as if I was washing my teeth and all the foam was on my mouth. He is asking £600 for it!'

That's just under £40,000 today.

Lady Ottoline Morrell provided friendship and a free lunch to the Bloomsbury group. She was a whip-sharp daughter of aristocracy with barely any education. She condemned herself for being 'stupid', yet would read Nietzsche, Stendhal, Proust, Sophocles, and said she read 17th-century philosopher Spinoza every day.

Morrell was a decade or so older than core members like Woolf, Bell, Grant. She lived in Bloomsbury during the crucial early years when the group formed, and she invited its members to her Thursday night gatherings at home. When Morrell moved to the Oxfordshire countryside, her house, Garsington Manor, played host to weekend parties, from which have come some of Bloomsbury's most recognizable images. Here's Lytton Strachey with Virginia Woolf at Garsington in 1923.

This is how it usually goes with Morrell: she's defined by what she provided to others. She was a sponsor of artists such as Augustus John and writers such as D. H. Lawrence, giving both money so they could survive and create. She was best friends with Strachey, and sometimes friends with Woolf. She was married to the Liberal MP Philip Morrell, and was mistress of the philosopher and mathematician Bertrand Russell.

That word! 'Mistress'. Morrell and Russell were both married when they began their relationship, and yet Morrell is the one cast in the subservient role of derogation. There is no male equivalent of 'mistress', and it does not work to say that Russell was Morrell's mistress – it implies feminization. This will be the only time I type it here.

Russell once wrote to Morrell that 'you need never have one instants doubt of your power to help me – you can help me more than you will ever realise, because you will think it all comes from me, when it is you reflected in me . . .'

Russell was Apostle number 224. As we've seen, the Apostles gathered weekly to talk ideas. They are considered great minds. Morrell gathered great minds weekly at her home, and she is considered a society hostess. Her life was full of these gendered traps.

Throughout it all, Morrell self-fashioned in garments that suited her, yet were increasingly anti-fashion. Her ostentatious leg-of-mutton sleeves and drama silhouettes ran counter to the slimline, simplified styles that emerged after World War I. What mattered was her own taste, her own self. 'Rise up – rise up,' she wrote in the first pages of her 1907 journal, 'fulfil the law of thy being – let all thy faculties have full play – open the prison doors – drive the imprisoned mind out – to walk – to run – to rejoice – to sing – gathering new strength, new energy on its way.'

Ottoline Violet Anne Cavendish-Bentinck was born in 1873, her family upper class, entrenched in the English aristocracy. Her father died young, aged 59, when she was five. Her half-brother, Arthur, inherited the title Duke of Portland, and with it, a grand house, Welbeck Abbey, in Nottinghamshire. Ottoline grew up there, living that feudal fantasy, made even more sweet by being given the title 'Lady'. When Ottoline was 16, Arthur married. A new duchess meant Ottoline and her mother moved out, becoming reliant on Arthur's allowances. This financial precarity would later bite her.

Her life at the Abbey had been lonely. Education meant learning the scriptures, and how to sew. Ottoline and her mother moved to a quiet house by secluded woods and lakes hidden away to the west of London.

Today, the area is a couple of hundred feet south of the M3 motorway, the major road out to the west of England, and a few hundred feet east of the M25, an orbital motorway that goes around the whole of London.

Heathrow Airport is not far north, and just the other side of the M3 is Thorpe Park, a theme park. My favourite rides are Saw, based on the horror film, and Stealth, the fastest rollercoaster in the United Kingdom.

In 1912, she revisited the neighbourhood, 'so full of poignant memories and awakenings,' she wrote in her journal. These awakenings were, on the surface, religious, but they have the fervour of the physical: 'such intense passionate asceticism,' she wrote, 'it was not hard except that the extreme self-denying was hard – and the loneliness was great.'

There was a counterpoint to this self-denial. 'And yet at the same time I loved my dresses – and made them – and was quite vain about these things,' she wrote. 'Apparently it didn't strike me that was wrong. My taste was very much the same as now in the way of clothes rather plain and long.'

From this young age, she was fashioning herself. Note too that description of her own dress sense, which is often talked about as bizarre, outlandish, extravagant, or worse. To Ottoline, it was 'plain and long'. Her clothes were tight: 'and shame on me I made myself ill by having too tight a dress.'

Here she is aged 16. Maybe the pose is meant to be open-mouthed surprise/delight, but it's like she can only just catch her breath.

That religious fervour, that 'intense passionate asceticism'. Imagine growing up female in a creaky social hierarchy, which casts women as objects of decoration/gratification/breeding, but you desire women. Religion itself can be restrictive, yet religious ecstasy could be a way of releasing all those otherwise inexpressible feelings. As we shall see, Ottoline was to bring religious fervour into her expressions of queer love.

In autumn 1896, aged 23, she travelled to Italy with her maid, Ellen, an older chaperone, Miss Rootes, and a new young friend, the Honourable Hilda Douglas-Pennant. 'We became great, and intimate, friends,' Ottoline wrote in her memoirs. For the trip, Morrell's luggage was mostly books, for which she didn't have enough room, so she 'put strong pockets all around the thick, full red cape I wore, into which I packed a rampart of books'. She continued, 'It made my cape extraordinarily heavy, and I had to walk with the utmost balance and care not to fall over. It was surprising and rather hard to anyone whom I happened to knock against.'

They travelled across Europe. By October, in Venice, Douglas-Pennant was eager for Morrell's undivided attention, and so the elderly Miss Rootes quit, leaving the three young women alone. They travelled together across Italy for the next five months. Douglas-Pennant introduced Morrell to Keats and Shelley. 'I drank then of the elixir of Italy,' Ottoline wrote. 'I drank so deeply of it that it has never left me.'

They returned home. I can find no photographs of Douglas-Pennant online. She lived to the age of 93, single her whole life.

In 1901, aged 28, Ottoline met an Etonian called Philip Morrell, who had discovered a fondness for collecting blue-and-white china at school. At the time, this was well-recognized queer code: in the late 1870s, Oscar Wilde had made the comment, 'I find it harder and harder every day to live up to my blue china.'

Morrell's father forced him to study law so he could join the family's law firm. Morrell hated it. He eventually set up his own law firm in London, but his interests lay elsewhere. With two friends, Logan Pearsall Smith and Percy Fielding, Morrell started an antiques company called Miss Toplady.

To spread the word, the three men printed business cards. Here is one, with its knowing camp text.

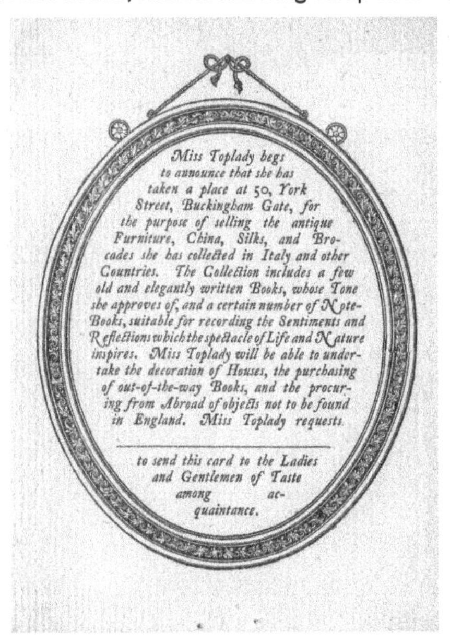

Miss Toplady begs to announce that she has taken a place at 50, York Street, Buckingham Gate, for the purpose of selling the antique Furniture, China, Silks, and Brocades she has collected in Italy and other Countries. The Collection includes a few old and elegantly written Books, whose Tone she approves of, and a certain number of Note-Books, suitable for recording the Sentiments and Reflections which the spectacle of Life and Nature inspires. Miss Toplady will be able to undertake the decoration of Houses, the purchasing of out-of-the-way Books, and the procuring from Abroad of objects not to be found in England. Miss Toplady requests

to send this card to the Ladies and Gentlemen of Taste among acquaintance.

In 1902, Ottoline and Philip married. Here is her wedding dress today, along with a little lace jacket, her petticoats, and a note, in her handwriting, pinned to her veil.

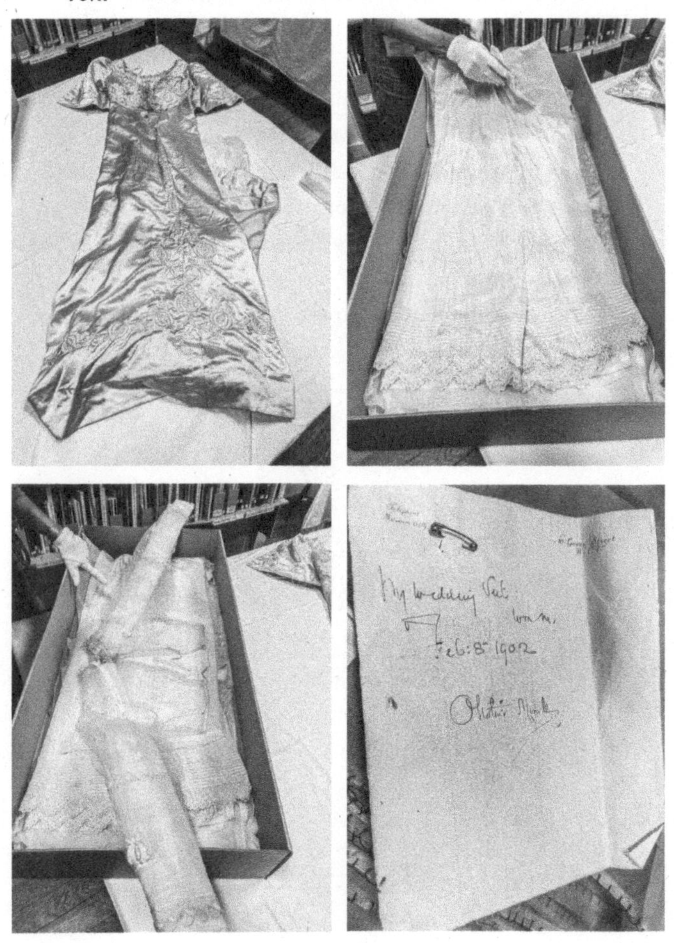

The couple had an open relationship, with other partners on both sides. Marriage was the constraint Morrell had to accept in order to live her queer life. In 1917, she would write, 'It was odd the day of my marriage as I stood at my bedroom door – a veil was lifted and I saw all down my future life – as looking down a river. Saw that I should have to bear a burden – and hold up our life in my arms – have to suffer – in silence. Oh how well I remember it.'

A photograph of Morrell from the year she married, protected by a cocoon of cloth. It's the swoop of the scarf, around the head then over the shoulder, but done loosely, at a distance from her face. It's the hat, it's the neckline, it's the look of contemplation – real or acted for the camera, it doesn't matter. The photograph is an act of self-fashioning, the misfit who dresses her own life. The photographer is unknown.

When she was 33, Morrell committed to the regular act of journal making. These are now in the British Library archives. One late-summer day, I held her first journal in my hands. It was small, aged, as if it had been soaked in tea, held by tied ribbons. She had written 'Mon Souvenirs' on the cover, with 'OM' beneath. I untied the ribbons.

The first line she wrote: 'Do not live in the past.' A paragraph later: 'Be what thou art, and not what thy imagination would like thee to be.'

Morrell has been described as 'Elizabethan', presumably for the exaggerated shoulder shape that she favoured. But this categorization doesn't fit with her own expressed desire to not live in the past. Morrell may have borrowed ideas from the past, but it was all to fashion an expression of herself as she really was. This was Morrell's own fashion, not the accepted, prescribed fashions of society. On 20 January 1907 she wrote, 'Conventionality is deadness.'

Morrell, that year.

There have been two biographies of Lady Ottoline Morrell, both written in the second half of the 20th century, when queerness was still not socially acceptable. In 1975's *Garsington Revisited*, Sandra Jobson Darroch wrote, 'there is no evidence that Ottoline ever had any Lesbian inclinations.' A new edition of the book, released in 2017, still included this line. In 1992, Miranda Seymour published her biography, titled *Ottoline Morrell: Life on a Grand Scale*. In it, she wrote, 'Lesbianism played no part in Ottoline's life.'

Morrell's journal says otherwise. Her handwriting is near impossible to read. Philip Morrell clearly wanted them understood. After her death in 1938, he had his secretary begin typing them up, with corrections in his own hand. The entries are so voluminous, the secretary was only up to 1925 when Philip Morrell himself died in 1943, and the transcriptions ended.

It took me a week to read all that had been transcribed. She is so quotable! I typed out 20,000 words of notes. There, right at the beginning, was this entry:

March 1907
The presence of a Friend. E.S.
Every time she comes – she fills me with Love. There must be a sacred space before and after Bless oh Lord this friendship and fill it with thyself.

Who was E.S.? Her husband had written the answer in tiny letters: 'Edith Sichel'. Sichel was a writer, who also helped destitute young female servants from the East End of London. She had a 'lifelong friendship' with Emily Ritchie, whom she met working for the Metropolitan Association for Befriending Young Servants. In 1889, Sichel and Ritchie moved to live in a cottage together in Surrey. They set up a home rescuing girls from an East End workhouse. Sichel spent half her income on the home.

Throughout her journal, Morrell would often mention her lovers by their initials, men like B.R. – Bertrand Russell. Sichel is only mentioned here once, as E.S. An undated letter from Sichel to Morrell states, 'I should love to have dinner (alone?) with you as you so sweetly suggest.'

And remember that teenage ecstasy of religious fervour that to me reads as code for queerness? Here are some more words from Morrell on Sichel via God: *If only it may increase and that each one of us might draw out and develop each other – I must not seek anything – only to give. And then, Grant that I may give of my best – and highest – of God's Light in me. Grant that we may be united in Thee.* Sounds like they were having fun. In this patriarchal society queer women were often invisible. Here's Sichel, passing through society in respectable, body-hiding clothes:

Morrell had no truck with this invisibility through conventional dressing. She wanted to express the fullness of herself. Another photograph of Morrell in 1907, the year of Sitchel. Morrell's garments are expressive, layered. There is purposeful choice behind the excess soft cloth leading to her wrist. It is like the folds of skin around an opening. The symbolism of the arum lilies seems pointed. They look like female sex.

There's only one mention of E.S. in the journal. I believe Morrell was keeping secrets, even though we assume journals are private and all-revealing. This is natural for someone living a life with queer layers hidden from a disapproving society, hiding even from themselves.

In 1906, the Morrells moved to 44 Bedford Square, on the lower west fringe of Bloomsbury. Philip had just become an MP and needed a London base. Ottoline was pregnant with twins: they needed a large family home. A boy, Hugh, died three days after birth. A girl, Julian, survived. Post-pregnancy, Morrell's health was poor. In 1907, she underwent a gynaecological operation. She could never have any more children.

In 1908, Morrell started her Thursday evening gatherings. Guests were invited to arrive after dinner for coffee and conversation. These are often cast as routine pleasantries of formal society, but under the guise of tradition, fresh social parameters were being set.

Morrell had become friends with Ethel Sands, a queer American artist living in London with her life partner, Nan Hudson. Sands came from money, and began hosting her own Thursday evenings at home for artists, writers, thinkers, politicians.

In September that year, Morrell made some decisions. They were about friends, clothes, patronage. 'This summer I gave up <u>work</u> to art – and friends,' she wrote, 'and perhaps I dare say it was happier – for I love friends – and feel that one might really make them one's "work".'

She then made a statement about clothing. 'One essential is not to spend too much <u>time</u> on dress – more important than not spending too much money.' No hours in front of the mirror for Morrell. She just wanted to throw on her body gorgeous expensive expressive things.

On the beach of the Lido in Venice that year, she draped herself in fabric, her pose showing she knew she was in front of the lens. The off-kilter tension of the cloth is like a late 20th-century gown of radical cutting by Vivienne Westwood, who exploded the elegance of construction.

Here was a queer woman, at the beginning of the 20th century, carving a pivotal role for herself at the intersections of contemporary culture and civic life.

In April 1909, Sands said to Morrell, 'Oh if you like it do it.' There is no sense they have had sex: Morrell said of Sands, 'Dear Ethel, she could not hug one!'

Look at this photograph of three queer clothed bodies: Sands, writer Henry James, Morrell. The hats have almost as wide a circumference as the skirts. Notice the mirroring of the two humans with active sex lives, their millinery in bloom. Then note the restriction of the self-declared celibate James's suit. How much would it have helped James from his gilded closet if he could have worn such a hat.

Out of all the figures in this book, Morrell was the first to express pacifist views. She was also the firmest in her convictions. In March 1909, she wrote that she and her husband were 'both so depressed at the military frenzy that has overtaken the country. It is all convention and the craze – the emotional craze that has urged on the man on the street just as a music hall singer would – amongst the people who think it is a Nation's smart set convention – as false as any other Public School convention.'

Her Thursday evenings gathered pace, Morrell writing that they were worth doing if they brought people together, letting them 'know each other better co-operate and help each other'. One April evening, E. M. Forster attended, 'and Miss Virginia Stephen came to meet him'. Morrell said Forster 'was like child' and that he was 'wriggling with joy when anything amused him'.

Like others who lived in Bloomsbury, Morrell also sought solitude away from the city. Here she wanders through long grass, her nightgown a rare loose garment. 'It is so delicious running on the grass with bare feet,' she once wrote, 'with only my nightgown on, and Soie running after me'. Soie was her pug, the name short for Socrates.

In the photo, it's clear she is enjoying self-fashioning, self-identifying, in front of the camera.

Morrell's journal gives us insight into the workings of fashion in 1909. Remember Lucile of London? The designer who was on the *Titanic*? Morrell had a coat by her! The Morrells went to an event at Hampton Court, a royal palace on the edge of London. 'Philip would make me dress very smart in my buff silk Lucile coat,' she said. In their party were two American women whose brown tailored clothes were 'very stiff' and 'ugly'.

Later that week, she went to see some fashion with Margot Asquith, the wife of the Prime Minister, H. H. Asquith – a Liberal and a philanderer. He had a thing for Morrell at the turn of the century, but she is not thought to have gotten involved. They went 'to see Paris Models,' wrote Morrell. This most likely means a static presentation on mannequins. In those days, what we would call a model they would call a 'mannequin'.

'It was a show of Poiret cloths,' Morrell continued.

We encountered Paul Poiret twice in the Woolf chapter: the French designer was cited as one of the first within fashion to move away from restrictive waists; he was the brother of Nicole Groult, who created an outfit for Woolf.

Here is a Poiret dress from 1910 in the collection of the Costume Institute of New York. A long column, it has an empire waist under the bust before going down to a slight gather below the knee. Poiret had just introduced the style, known as the hobble skirt.

He was releasing fashion from corsetry. Now he was just making it hard for women to walk.

Morrell did not like the crowd drawn to the show. 'All the horrid hard smart ladies of London were there,' she wrote, 'How wooden and uninteresting they make themselves.' But she liked the clothes. 'The Fashions were very Empire, and very lovely.' She was tempted by the cloaks, and wanted to buy one, but she took Philip to see them next day 'and the temptation vanished'.

There was drama. Apparently the Poiret show was in an official space. 'This caused a great deal of trouble for Margot,' wrote Morrell of the Prime Minister's wife, 'as The English Shops objected to her using a Government building for French dressmakers.' Morrell then attempted patriotism by going to see the wares at 'Jay'. It's likely she meant Jay's London: there's a Jay's London dress from 1908 in the V&A collection. But apart from a shawl, 'I don't want anything.' She then made a declaration. 'I do want so much to dress totally plainly and unfashionably – in just loose flowing things – which will drape me.'

Morrell, a year later, draped.

A letter from Grant to Keynes, written on 3 July 1910, gives crucial insights into the Morrells, their clothes and their open marriage. Grant had been with them, presumably at a Thursday night gathering. He wrote that Ottoline looked 'superb in a magnificent gown of grey clinging material with a red rose at her bosom'. Philip 'was clothed in a chocolate coloured suit', with 'a low white brocade waistcoat with turquoise buttons, a soft white shirt, striped socks & patent leather shoes'. For an MP, whose days were spent straight-laced at the House of Commons, these were wildly fancy at-home and in-private garments.

Grant had to leave early. He regretted it, 'as afterwards, I hear, they discussed all their affairs, sodomitical, ordinary & sapphic.' Not only was their marriage queer and open, it was also open for conversation. They told all, and, as we can see from Grant's letter, the gossip from the evening quickly spread.

'Ottoline owned up to several passions for women, & Philip to an affair only a year ago with a young man. He said, however, that now he was rather ashamed of it, as he now considered him to be both ugly & rather vulgar. He went on to say that he had observed that unnatural passions among men were violent but shortlived.'

That year, Philip lost his seat in Henley, but won an election as MP for Burnley in Lancashire. He would remain in Parliament as a Liberal MP until 1918. If his queerness had been discovered, his career would have been destroyed, which may be why he couched his confessions as 'unnatural passions'.

In February 1911, Ottoline was reading Colette, a queer French writer who had recently published *The Vagabond*. When discussing it in her journal, Morrell reveals her lack of interest in male/female penetrative sex. 'Men say – it is always in women's eye – the thought of and desire for physical contact,' she wrote. Morrell often used 'physical' when she meant sex, 'but I believe most women really think it is brutal. They do long for love and devotion and tenderness – and passion – certainly. Must the brutal side always have to be accepted with these? Men wish always to be masters of the women they love – and they think that it is accomplished thus.'

Morrell then quoted from *The Vagabond*, in French. I put it into Google Translate: 'I tasted in her,' the translation read, 'this protective mood, this skill in caring for women who sincerely and passionately loved women.'

A couple of weeks later, Bertrand Russell came to stay. It was the beginning of a seven-year on-off relationship, during which they would share around 2,500 letters.

Morrell, the year she quoted from Colette and started seeing Russell. The photograph was taken by her husband. That luscious drape and swing of cloth, working to enhance and decorate the curves and lines of the body.

Russell was in deep. Morrell, not so much. In September 1912 she wrote, 'I feel nothing is more awful than to receive so much from B.R.,' using his initials, as we saw earlier with Edith Sichel, 'and yet to be able to give so little in comparison in return. Always to stand outside a land that would be bliss to enter – and yet never to be <u>inside</u> – and there he stands dragging me – drawing me in.'

And then later that month: 'I had it so strongly yesterday

as if my whole being longed to kiss someone – and yet no _one_ person that I know.' It sounds like a desire for cruising, that queer and elemental instinct for consensual, liberated, anonymous pleasure.

Their first break-up came in September 1913. Russell had written to Morrell 'saying his love for me – is cold – or gone'. She had nothing to say to him, 'but to open my hands and let the bird fly free – which I have done.' A few weeks later, she commented, 'One's character is like a casket of jewels – false or real precious stones – some to be worn and polished – some to be thrown away as rubbish.'

The approach of war horrified Morrell. Her husband spoke against it in the House of Commons on 2 August 1914. She described his lone voice as 'the last public word for Peace'. A few days later, she wrote, 'Is it patriotic to ruin the well-being of your own country and that of the country you are fighting. Is it patriotic to overthrow all social reforms – national progress – that has been slowly and painfully building up.' Her list continued. 'Is it above all patriotic to lie and lie – and worst of all lie to ourselves and say that we are fine and self-sacrificing.'

Her London home became a haven for pacifists and artists. New faces appeared, such as artists Carrington and Brett, who both went by surname only, both wore cropped hair and corduroy pants, with 'Ottoline herself at the head of a troupe of short haired young ladies from the Slade prancing about,' wrote Vanessa Bell.

Her Thursday evenings had moved on from the formality of conversation: music played, there was dancing, and Vanessa Bell wrote that guests were 'looking as beautiful as they could in clothes seized from Ottoline's drawers'. She clearly didn't mind others wearing what she owned.

Remember when Vanessa Bell suggested to Roger Fry that they hold an Omega Workshops 'dress parade' fashion show at Morrell's? It was during this period: 'Ottoline has a dressmaker who drinks but is otherwise capable and who could work under me,' wrote Bell.

Around this time, the Morrells bought Garsington, a 17th-century manor house near Oxford. Ottoline moved there in the spring of 1915, the manor then becoming a refuge for conscientious objectors.

The scene in this photograph at Garsington from 1915 looks stilted. It's the waistcoats worn by Strachey and Grant, and the gendered imbalance: man pontificating, women silent receivers. That's Morrell on the far left, next to her Maria Nys, a queer Belgian refugee who would eventually marry Aldous Huxley. Grant is standing behind, his hands crossed over his crotch, just like in those photos with Keynes. To the right is Vanessa Bell, looking bored out of her mind.

Morrell was not silent. On Easter Sunday 1916, the Prime Minister, H. H. Asquith, arrived at Garsington. She commandeered him, saying, '"you know I am a rebel. I am very much in sympathy with the conscientious objectors" – and I went on to tell them all about them.'

Imagine a 21st-century Prime Minister spending the weekend with today's equivalent of conscientious objectors – say, Extinction Rebellion. They would likely not survive the political fallout.

A few weeks later, Morrell was talking with Asquith about Ireland, where the Easter Rising had just occurred. 'How mad England is to treat Ireland as they do,' Morrell wrote. In June, an Irish diplomat, Roger Casement, was put on trial for high treason in London. 'I shall always see in Asquith – a murderer,' wrote Morrell during the trial. Casement was executed on 3 August. The night before, Morrell wrote, 'I hate Asquith and all the callous sensual men who let a man like that die – quite casually – they are not human. They are made of india rubber – with sexual organs – no hearts.'

Garsington was made modern by the female gaze, the female body. The artist Brett moved into what Morrell called 'Conscience Cottage' at the Manor, taking residence there throughout the war. On 8 October 1916, Morrell wrote of Brett in her journal:

'I love her very much. She is wonderful and has passionate love – the love that I love to know and that I give too. I wish people knew this love – life is so dull without it. It is not selfish love. It is love – love.'

Morrell took this photograph of Brett a year later.

Morrell, arm-in-arm with Brett at Garsington. Beside them is the poet Siegfried Sassoon, with whom Morrell had just become friends. She had a crush on Sassoon. He occupied much mental chatter space in her journal, even though he was queer and, at that time, pursuing men.

Morrell's anti-fashion stance was becoming more pronounced. As her younger friends pushed into garments of cleaner line, her silhouettes became more dramatic. It was dressing as maximal expression: flounce, drape and gather part of her own self-determination.

That summer Brett painted *Umbrellas*, with Morrell at the centre of its swirl of activity, the drape of her dress acting like energy lines that activate all around. The figure on the right is Strachey.

Into her twenties, Brett described herself as 'virgin', which I believe we can interpret as a sexually active queer woman who had not had penetrative sex with a man. Morrell would write of her, 'Sometimes I think poor Brett is "wanting". All these virgin ladies get so small – so intensely over interested in small details – in material things. No wide outlook. It may partly be virginity but more even from not living enough with men – not having their minds knocked about enough by men's minds.' In 1924, Brett would move to Taos, New Mexico, USA, where she would spend the rest of her life. It was a haven for queer creative women, far from the patriarchal trap that assumed a woman's mind needed to be knocked about by a man's.

In 1917, the terms of the Morrells' open marriage were tested. Philip told Ottoline he was expecting children by two different women. She was OK with his affairs, but was blindsided by this news. Their marriage continued. On August 4, she wrote in her journal: 'Grow steel within you -- cut your desire down -- cut your way onward.' On 27 August, 'The bird in my breast must escape.'

That summer, Morrell took photographs of Carrington naked, including this one of her climbing a statue. Morrell kept a copy in her photo album. This is the print that Morrell gave to Carrington, which is found in her album.

In Carrington's album, above this naked photo sits a torn photograph of Morrell, seen over the page. It's like the tear matches the chosen angles of her dress's layered design.

Morrell's naked photographs of Carrington are now widely known, though it is rarely mentioned that it was Morrell who took them. Carrington also defined herself as 'virgin', but it doesn't feel too much of a leap to assume she and Ottoline were making out.

A year earlier, Carrington wrote to Morrell. 'You know how much I have enjoyed myself, so it is useless for me to try & write you an eloquent letter of thanks or express my extreme misery at having to leave you.' Later in the letter she wrote, 'I am so full of affection for you this morning that I cannot write properly.' And then, 'I felt like writing you a marvellous letter like sunshine on the water.'

The sign off:

still Pug. Pug. Pug.
and again Pug. Pug. Pug.

The same summer that Morrell photographed Carrington naked, Morrell was also photographed naked, also in the grounds of Garsington. The photographer is unknown. Clothes are strewn on the grass path behind. Were they shed instinctively, or placed artfully there in the light, out of the shadow, to send a particular message about what we wear, and the body beneath?

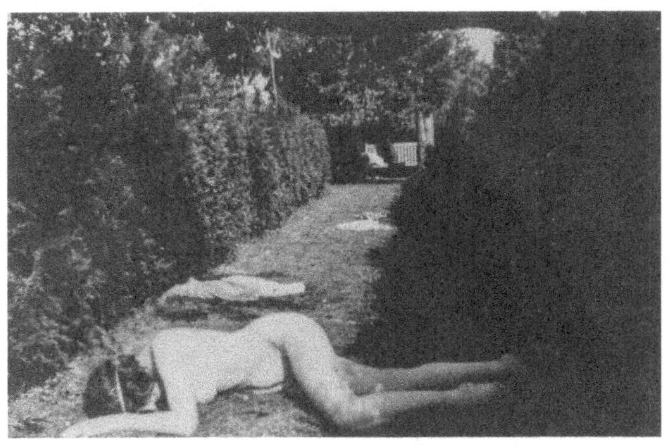

In June 1917, Roger Fry wrote to Vanessa Bell. He was on a train, so had to switch halfway from ink pen to pencil.

Ott. in his text means Ottoline. 'Poor dear,' wrote Fry, 'what an affliction to have Ott. upon you – couldn't you keep her off? She and Virginia have fallen into each other's arms and each flatters t'other to the top of their bents.'

He continued: 'What a lot of temporary mischief it'll brew, that liaison – I s'pose it'll cut me off. Virginia and Ott. will get in some fine whacks at you, too. But it won't last long.'

The letter is usually overlooked or brushed aside. That phrase 'fallen into each other's arms' has been interpreted to mean they have formed an alliance of temporary convenience in a gossip war, like two embattled cast members of the *Real Housewives* reality TV franchise.

And yet Fry describes it as a 'liaison'. He knew Woolf and Morrell were long acquainted. On 18 May 1911, Fry and Woolf accompanied each other to a Thursday evening at Morrell's. Also present was Winston Churchill.

Maybe what Fry means in this letter is exactly what he says, that it was a liaison between two queer women which he thought wouldn't last long. Maybe, that summer in 1917, they were actually in each other's arms.

For evidence, let's look back. In May 1909, Vanessa Bell had written to Woolf. 'Is Ottoline becoming my rival in your affections? I am suspicious. You will have a desperate liaison with her I believe, for I rather think she shares your Sapphist tendencies and only wants a little encouragement.' Bell continued, 'She once told me that she much preferred women to men and would take any trouble to get to know a woman she liked, but would never do the same for a man.'

A couple of days before, Woolf had written to Violet

Dickinson, the woman who had stirred her volcano. 'Ottoline is slowly growing rather fond of me. It is like sitting beneath an Arum lily; with a thick golden bar in the middle, dropping pollen, or whatever that is which seduces the male bee.' Arum lilies, just like those in that photograph of Morrell from 1907.

Morrell enjoyed being with Woolf. 'I thought Virginia wonderful and very much more developed since I had last seen her,' she wrote in 1910, 'much more natural and full blooded and human.'

Woolf was often absent that decade due to her struggles with mental ill-health. Towards the end of the war, Woolf was recovering enough to begin seeing friends again. Morrell broke the ice first by writing to Woolf. 'It was a great surprise and pleasure to see your hand again,' Woolf replied. 'I haven't forgotten you – indeed you have become one of the romantic myths of my life.' What did Woolf mean by 'romantic'? I could not see it used in her published letters to other correspondents written around this time. She saved it just for Morrell. Maybe 'romantic' means 'romantic'.

Woolf agreed to come for tea. 'My images, after leaving you,' Woolf then wrote to Morrell, 'were all of the depths of the sea – mermaid Queens, shells, the bones of the shipwrecked. I was incapacitated for normal life for some time after seeing you.'

Morrell invited the Woolfs to stay at Garsington. Woolf wrote, 'Please don't treat me as an invalid – save for breakfast in bed (which is now a luxury and not a necessity) I do exactly as others do.'

Woolf at the breakfast table, not in bed, at Garsington, taken by Morrell. It is thought to be from 1917.

In an October letter, Woolf writes, 'you don't realise, at least I sometimes think you don't, how nice it is to see you – not only romantic, but nice.' A week later, Woolf wrote to Morrell about seeing her at 'Roger's tea party', presumably Roger Fry. 'The walk in the rain was romantic and so satisfactory from my point of view – but then I like you yourself, beneath the depressions and agitations and varieties of the surface.' She continued: 'By this time surely, our degree of polish is scratched through, and we have come upon something – I have, anyhow – human and true beneath.'

Woolf talked about visiting with Leonard the next month. 'Do you mind our having no clothes?' She said they lived like 'superior mechanics'.

Morrell's mentions of Woolf continued to be warm. 'A delightful letter from Virginia today,' she wrote on 1 May 1919, 'a cold eternal virgin.' That word again. A few days later, Morrell was invited to Woolf's home for dinner. 'She is exquisitely lovely,' wrote Morrell, and then, 'she is very attractive and delightful – and very witty and entrancing.'

Morrell was clearly distracted. 'When I was on my way to the station I felt my head and found I had forgotten my hat!' she wrote, but, luckily, 'No one noticed as it was night.'

The next month, Woolf would write that passage in her own diary about being badly dressed, yet Morrell had just described her as exquisitely lovely, attractive, delightful, entrancing. It is as if Morrell saw her.

Morrell's gaze was often on herself. This photograph is from either 1920 or 1921, the pose like a fashion shoot.

It looks like one of the velvet dresses I saw at the Fashion Museum in Bath.

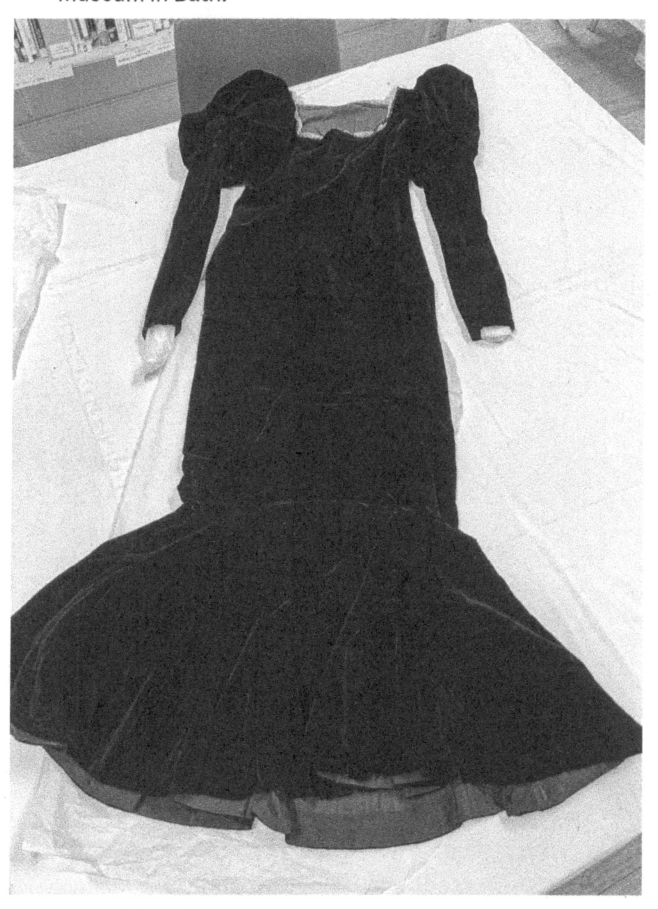

Those big shoulders were wildly unfashionable at the time. Morrell loved them, as she did a squared and decorated neckline. Here's a satin gown, its wider waist suggests it's from when Morrell was older and heavier.

We know that Woolf and Morrell had a long-term close friendship, one that included falling 'into each other's arms'. We know that Morrell thought Woolf was beautiful. We know that both were queer women.

There's contradictory evidence too. Woolf had long made sport of being vile about Morrell in letters. In July 1918, Woolf spent a contented weekend at Garsington, but then described Morrell as a 'poor old ninny'. Woolf's vilest jibes at Morrell came in 1924, calling her 'a ship with its sails rateaten, & its masts mouldy, & green serpents on the decks'. This vivid imagery is often taken as proof of Woolf's general fickleness toward Morrell. But wait: at that time Woolf was having her head turned by Vita Sackville-West. She was in the throes of wild new passion. Morrell was old news.

I would not be surprised if Morrell and Woolf were lovers, at some point, in some form. At least, let's consider them queer comrades. What do comrades do? They help each other out.

Remember that *Vogue* portrait of 1924, the one where Woolf is supposedly wearing her mother's dress?

In 1927, Morrell had her portrait taken by Maurice Beck and Helen MacGregor, the photographers who had taken Woolf's portrait for *Vogue*.

Morrell was 6 foot tall. Woolf was 5 foot 7 inches. We know from Bell's letter in 1915 that Morrell was happy for others to wear her clothes. We know that both women did not fully reveal their queerness in their diaries: so much went unwritten.

Woolf's dress in the *Vogue* shoot is clearly too big for her. Ostentatious shoulders. A squared and decorated neck. Satin. Rather than Woolf wearing her mother's dress, maybe she was wearing a dress from another woman for whom she had great affection. We've already seen, with

Forster and el Adl, how queer partners can wear the same garments to manifest their love. I have no evidence other than my eyes, but for this *Vogue* shoot, it looks to me like Woolf is wearing one of Morrell's dresses.

Let's luxuriate a little longer in Morrell's clothes. As this book was about to go to print, a surprise. I was tipped off by Gill MacGregor, a costume mounter, maker and researcher: some of Morrell's dresses could be by the Venetian designer Fortuny. I contacted the Museo Fortuny and they confirmed this embroidered, pleat-sided dress was a fake. Whatever, Morrell left it filthy.

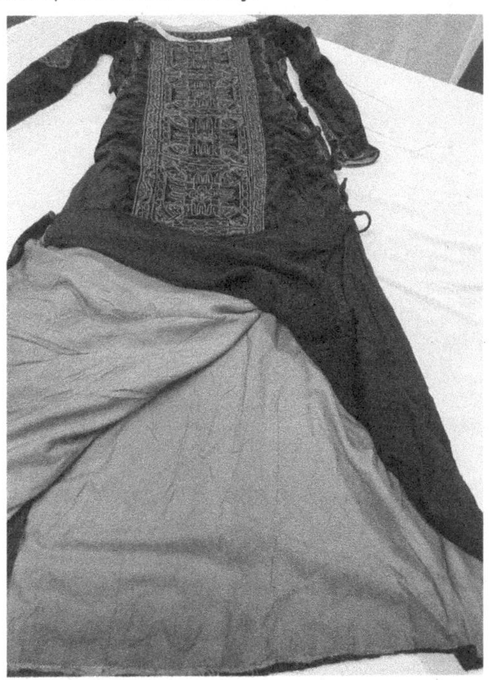

But this gauze gown: I found an exact match of the print. Museo Fortuny agreed it was genuine. Sudden glorious fashion.

This devoré velvet dress has the simplicity of 1920s fashion, but with Morrell's preference for a puffed-up shoulder.

Was Morrell turning demure? Not a chance. The width of the waist suggests this next dress was worn when Morrell was in later life, the extremity and vivacity of pattern and silhouette only increasing with age.

One more garment: a pair of velvet pants made in Paris. They are fabulous: this tension, created by a slender waist, legs that head out to about twice the diameter, before a cropped length, held stiff and proud by the luscious cloth.

Morrell left some cigarettes in one of the pockets. The tobacco is now just dust.

Bloomsbury, fashion, philosophy

For a while, Bloomsbury was out of fashion. Woolf's reputation dissipated after World War II, eventually to be recovered by the research and writing of feminists in the 1970s.

Fashion in art shifted too. After the second world war, New York became the focus of the art world, with its abstract expressionism and its Pop. Older British artists could feel left behind. Eventually, Duncan Grant and Vanessa Bell were pretty much forgotten.

When Grant died in 1978, Charleston was in a desperate state. Woolf's home, Monk's House, had been under the ownership of the University of Sussex. I was told that visiting academics were sometimes put up there, as if it were an Airbnb.

Bloomsbury needed time, air, space, distance. It has become fashionable again. The work of its individuals can now be considered for what it is.

As we saw with Kim Jones and Dior, when fashion designers draw on Bloomsbury for inspiration, they often do so for ideas, rather than copying a way of dressing.

In June and September 2019, Comme des Garçons staged two fashion shows based on *Orlando*. Comme des Garçons is the label of Rei Kawakubo, a Japanese designer whose career has been a continual search for new expression through clothing.

Because of the industry's scheduling, the men's collection, Comme des Garçons Homme Plus, was revealed first. Over the page, the opening look.

Kawakubo combined 20th-century design tropes – a tailored jacket, a simple dress – to express Orlando's freedom from gender.

Three months later, Kawakubo revealed the women's collection. Here is a look from mid-way through the show.

Kawakubo pushes beyond our normal understanding of clothes. She also resists explaining her work. It is all there to see. To me, this outfit expresses interior states – how we feel within ourselves – or maybe Orlando's seven-day cocoon-like trance in Woolf's novel, during which the character transitions.

The collections came about because Kawakubo had been asked by composer Olga Neuwirth to create costumes for a new opera, *Orlando*, staged at the Vienna State Opera. The costumes themselves were distinct from Kawakubo's *Orlando* catwalk collections.

Woolf's novel provided a space within which Kawakubo could forge expression. This has been my experience of researching the Bloomsbury group. While doing so, I have been able to think about clothing in new, expansive ways.

Fashion writing is usually caught up in constant forward cycles, hungry for the imminent novelty of catwalk seasons that are always six months ahead of the outside world. It means fashion thinking can get stuck in a world of promises rather than reality. Looking back a hundred years has been like putting an oar hard in the water. No longer is my thinking about clothes dominated by this forward motion. What matters is experiencing the individual, in their moment, the tension of being alive.

I was a fashion critic for many years. Often, when I was trying to capture the essence of a successful garment, I would talk about its tension, to express how its components worked together. Or, indeed, I would try to pinpoint an unsuccessful garment's lack of tension. The word was a way for me to break from fashion speak, and to get to the heart of the matter.

That sense of tension has long been part of how I understand clothes. In January, I did some teaching at the London College of Fashion. When I was suggesting to one student how they could resolve the design of a garment, I mentioned tension. The student asked, what did I mean?

At the time I was reading Wittgenstein, the queer, troubled, impenetrable, elucidating philosopher, who was Apostle number 252.

Wittgenstein believed 'everything that can be thought at all can be thought clearly. Everything that can be put into words can be put clearly.' And yet the fashion industry makes its profit from '*je ne sais quoi*'. It relies on a sense of mystery and allure to keep consumers wanting to buy its secrets.

But what if, actually, '*je sais quoi*'. What if we *can* know. What if there is no mystery to fashion at all. What if, with this knowledge, we can still appreciate design. We can just do so no longer hoodwinked by the fashion industry's smoke and mirrors.

Wittgenstein once wrote in his notes, 'how hard I find it to see what is right in front of my eyes!' Those foundational years of the Bloomsbury group were about thinking and speaking plainly. To answer the student's question about tension, I realized I should do the same. I needed to see what was in front of my own eyes. I needed to look at tension. My notebook, from that day.

Imagine I'm writing a paper for The Apostles, or for a Bloomsbury gathering. Its title:

<u>Tension and a new philosophy of fashion.</u>

I want to understand my clothing. By this I mean that I want a genuine understanding of what I wear and why I wear it, not just assumed knowledge handed down or picked up, a language of fashion that carries authority but is rarely interrogated. I live in my clothes. I want to live fully. I cannot live fully if I do not understand what I live in.

For this to be possible, we must evolve a new philosophy of fashion. We need new linguistic tools to try and unpick what Virginia Woolf called 'frock consciousness'. She wrote in her diary, 'Still I cannot get at what I mean'. We can now try and help her.

This is necessary because the current language of fashion is inadequate for the task. Our common method of discussing clothes is through archetypes of garments – coats, jackets, dresses, trousers etc. By 'archetypes', I mean both the ideal models of which all others are copies, and also the mental images that pervade our collective unconscious, as described by psychiatrist Carl Jung.

'The fact is,' Jung wrote in *The Archetypes and the Collective Unconscious*, 'that all archetypal images are so packed with meaning in themselves that people never think of asking what they really do mean.' Jung goes on to say, the 'he' here meaning humans in general, that 'when he starts thinking of them, he does so with the help of what he calls "reason" – which in point of fact is nothing more than the sum-total of all his prejudices and myopic views.'

It's how we are with clothes. Tailoring, for example,

carries archetypal meanings of power, authority, masculinity; all meanings generated by 'prejudices and myopic views'.

These archetypes are often grouped, organized or explained by trends, informed by fashion history as well as contemporary culture. These can be broad trends that evolve over decades, such as the 21st-century shift from formal to informal clothing, driven by relaxation of working conditions. Trends can also be seemingly random and over-in-a-flash: as I write, for instance, fashion is coming out of a brief enthusiasm for crop-tops. It is moving towards dressed-up notions of elegance. When this book is published, when it is read, this will likely have changed.

Trends can seem like an easy way to understand garments or styles, but they put us at a remove. By discussing a garment through a trend, we are discussing it through a preconceived idea, approaching it as an archetype. We are talking about the idea of the thing, rather than the actual garment itself. It is like Plato's allegory of the cave, in *The Republic*. Trends are like the shadows on the wall. Seeking knowledge through them mean staying in the dark.

Our new philosophy needs to cut away this reliance on trends entirely, while also being able to explain why we humans have, for millennia, based our understanding of fashion upon them. 'And so our state and yours will be really awake,' wrote Plato, 'and not merely dreaming like most societies today, with their shadow battles and their struggles for political power, which they treat as some great prize.'

A good starting point would be to look for a unifying quality that would define all garments. Most qualities of garments can be immediately rejected, since they clearly do not apply to all clothes. There is no universal cut, fit, design, material, colour. It cannot be said that garments are designed to protect or keep the body warm, since a garment can be made from a sliver of cloth. Such slivers of cloth, exposing parts of the body that most would keep concealed, discount the moralistic notion that garments are there to protect modesty.

It cannot even be said that 'every garment is something worn on the body', since garments can be produced but never worn by any human, like the endless tons of unsold product from fashion brands that are sent to landfill.

We need a fresh approach to find our unifying quality, one that tries to understand the garments themselves, as well as the ways in which humans relate to and engage with them. We need to think about a garment's very state of being. This leads us to the idea of tension.

Every single garment can be described in terms of tension. That's every garment ever made, and that ever will be made.

This tension takes many forms, from the nature of the cloth itself and the construction of the garment, to its visual effects, contrasts and harmonies, and its interpersonal and societal messaging.

1) Material tension: Garments have an inherent tension that begins with their materials. This is a tension that we take so much for granted, we never think of it. Take a cotton T-shirt. Cotton fibres are twisted together to make the yarn, that yarn woven to make the cloth, which is held together from the moment of weaving by tension. This tension exists from

the first moment the yarn is twisted together, until the fabric finally decomposes to soil, whenever that may be.

Cotton cloth becomes a cotton T-shirt through the creation of tension. Pattern pieces are sewn together, the stitches taut to hold the garment securely. This is even before a body wears the garment and brings its own strains to these stitches.

2) Design tension: Fashion emerges from the interplay between a garment's constituent parts, particularly the relationship between details. This can be elemental, like the scale of a cotton T-shirt's ribbing at the neck, the positioning of its shoulder seam, its length: how these balance, play off each other, is what makes us desire a particular design.

   When any garment is made, visual tensions – shapes and angles and contrasts – arise from its cut, fit, construction. Good tension – either harmonious balance or intentional imbalance – is what creates good design.

3) Societal tension: Through our garments, we send messages to each other, creating tensions within the societal structure that we navigate daily. Often this manifests as very real tension – conflicts of values and interests, even physical conflict – particularly when it comes to the messaging from clothes of authority, power or control.

4) Economic and environmental tension: We may not think about it when we get dressed in the morning, but the production of clothing dominates the planet. At the time of writing, Bernard Arnault, CEO of LVMH and owner of luxury fashion brands, such as Louis Vuitton, Dior and Celine, is the richest human in the world. Meanwhile, according to the World Wide Fund for Nature, cotton is 'the most

widespread profitable non-food crop in the world'. Most cotton garments have entailed exploitation and ecological damage in some form: who picked the cotton, what are the conditions of their lives, what is the effect on the soil, how much natural forest was cleared, how much water used, how much pollution created, who profits, who looks away?

The *Oxford English Dictionary* lists many definitions of tension, including this: 'The conflict created by interplay of constituent elements of a work of art. Used esp. of poetry.' I would like to add to this definition: 'also true of fashion'.

The evening before I wrote this, I made a new top. I sewed its pieces together on the machine. The stitches, previously just thread, now created tension by piercing, knotting and looping to hold the garment in place.

Construction is like alchemy to me, the manipulation of 2D pattern pieces to become a 3D form. Pinning and then sewing the sleeve, the flat fabric takes on life and character, inviting the body in. It is so simple, and it is a wonder.

I am wearing the new top to write these words. As I write, its stitches are ready to take the strain of being worn. The ribbed collar stays in place; the shoulder seams hold their line; the sleeves withstand the action of my arms. Again, I take this tension for granted. If the stitches did not maintain tension, the top would fall apart.

This is the background tension that is in every single piece of clothing. It is fundamental, present in even the most mundane design. But I wanted something more. When I cut the pieces of cloth, I intentionally stoked the contrast between the front and the back. I followed the same thinking as for the first two tops that I made, only this time

I cut the back longer by an extra 60 cm. The front panel sits at my hips. The curved back touches mid-calf.

There is clear tension between the regularly cut front, and this long back behind it. There is also tension in the way the back cuts into the front, with its diagonal lined sides that start beneath the armholes and end in front of the hips. As with my first two tops, the front is hugged by the back. A hug is a hold of tension.

Here's the top.

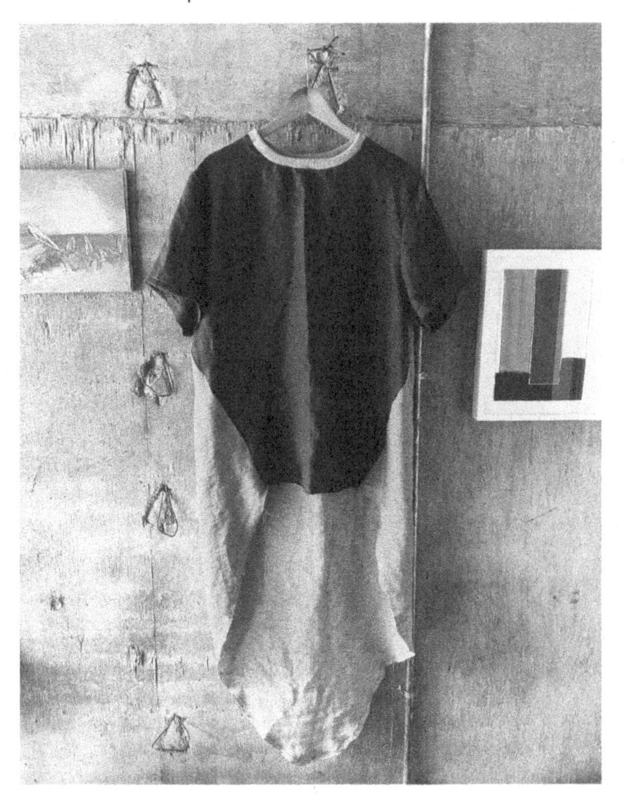

The curved back is like that of a morning coat, but it's also like a dress. Yet it's not. It's something else.

It wasn't till I'd finished that I realized what I'd done. The front is blue, the back is pink. In the 20th century, these colours became gendered. Following World War II, pink started to be seen as a female colour, encouraged by a return to traditionally gendered roles after women had worked traditionally male jobs during the conflict. Men had come back from fighting, they wanted their jobs again; women were sent home, forced into subservience once more. Pink was used to make this subservience pretty, and then to sell the idea of domesticity and motherhood to the next generations of girls. Blue was for boys.

Following these notions – pink for female, blue for male – I'd made a top that reflected how I felt in the fuzz of 21st-century gender identification: presenting as male, but with a swell of female all around me. The maleness in me is all front. I'm OK with presenting as male. I find it funny. But that maleness in me is the minority. The femaleness is the background, less prominent, but spanning a larger surface area.

I'm entering my fifties. Now is the time to understand this tension within me, to express it, and to allow it. A way to express this tension, to acknowledge and understand it, is through clothing. The two colours bounce off each other. The collar is cut from ribbing in a muddier pink, like it is bridging the two.

My new top is an extreme of tension. But tension in fashion can be so low-key that it barely registers: the placing of buttons, the size of them; the width of a collar, a line of stitching. It may be more brazen, like the sudden shock of a mini-skirt or a pair of shorts, or a flowing, loose silhouette when fashion has been dominated by garments that are fitted and tight.

The fashion industry relies on these abrupt switches in tension to create novelty, and thus drive consumption. You've only got skinny leg jeans? You need wide leg! Your wardrobe is all pastels? You need vivids! OK now you need black! It goes on and on.

Tension is personal. When I think about clothes, I first think about myself, before I consider how others will see me. Wearing this top to write these words, I am buoyed by the expanse of blue in my lower field of vision. I'm looking directly at my laptop, where these words are appearing as I type, but the lower 10 per cent of my field of vision is all blue. By wearing this top, I am giving myself this experience. Like Lady Ottoline Morrell, I'm wearing this to please myself.

When Woolf wrote to Eliot to say he should 'bring no clothes', she was puncturing the rigid hierarchy that garments maintained in society. It was a request for him to disarm himself. Woolf once commented that Eliot was so uptight, it was like he wore a 'four-piece suit', as if the three regular pieces weren't enough. She was asking him to let go, to find a tension of his own.

With each member of the Bloomsbury group we've encountered, we've experienced different forms of tension.

Woolf's tension was the duality that she expressed so eloquently: her hatred of fashion balanced against a fascination with clothes. With her sister Vanessa, she bore the burden that comes from an abusive upbringing; the strain of growing up within a restrictive, oppressive society.

In her adult life, Bell embraced the creative tension that comes with going your own way, which included making her own clothes. I felt it last night, when I made this top, getting myself ready to write these words.

The tension of Duncan Grant's clothes was in their release and removal; he was barely able to keep them on his body. E. M. Forster and John Maynard Keynes were caught in the tension of tailoring: Forster desperate to escape it, Keynes exploiting it for power and influence. Lady Ottoline Morrell whipped up her own kind of tension, increasingly at odds with the mode of the time, through her attempt to express herself to those around her.

While we've been talking about Bloomsbury, clothes, philosophy, what we've really been talking about is the tension within humans and between humans, and the primal role that clothing plays in navigating that tension. That 'tension' could also be called love.

Clothes are at the heart of how we experience ourselves; they provide the subconscious messaging that gives us knowledge of another human before they speak, if we ever even hear them speak. This tension is often considered a mystery because it happens without words, but we can know it.

Imagine waking up one day and dressing without preconception, in response to your body, its physical needs, as well as your desire for expression. This would be answering Woolf's call to 'bring no clothes'. How would you express your character through garments? By character, I don't mean the layer we present to the world, but our inner tensions that may remain unexpressed, our own poetry.

For many, this is an impossibility. Some may need to

dress a certain way for work, or otherwise jeopardize their employment and source of income. Some may live in society where true self-expression risks discrimination, violence or even threat to life.

But for many others – those who work from home, or within creative industries, or liberal societies – dressing without preconception is more possible than before. If we are to bring no clothes, we must do so without submitting to archetypes and their prejudiced or myopic meanings.

If we understand and wield the various tensions in our clothes, we can begin to dress without preconception. If we begin to dress without preconception, we can begin to remove the societal prejudices that clothing helps to maintain.

This understanding of tension goes beyond ourselves. By considering the tension in the garments of others, we can get closer to the human beneath.

On the last Sunday in August, I took a walk to Bloomsbury. I was wearing my new top with the blue front and long pink back. It was still hot, but there was breeze in the air. As I walked, the train of my top flowed out behind me. I cut through backstreets and got to Brunswick Square.

By the gate was a board that detailed who had lived where at various times: the Woolfs, Grant and Maynard Keynes at No. 38; Forster at Nos. 26 and 27. At a tree near the sign, a mother was helping her son go to the toilet. She had two teenage daughters with her. One was wandering off.

'Go sit down on the bench,' shouted the mother. The teenager was in a cropped vest, her stomach showing. The cropped vest, its daring and its display, had the tension of rebellion, of independence, of imminent adulthood, whether the mother approved or not.

I walked over to the Brunswick Plane, a tree planted around 1796, the second oldest of its species in the city. By me walked three generations of the same family: grandparents, a parent and a child. The grandmother was closest to me, a vape pen gripped in her right hand. She wore a black T-shirt that had printed on it the following mantra:

VERY LIKEABLE
VERY LIKEABLE
VERY LIKEABLE
VERY LIKEABLE

It's not clear if the words were meant to convince herself or those around her. The mantra was manifesting tension.

I headed to Tavistock Square. The Woolfs lived there between the wars. An older man was sitting on a bench in a camouflage jacket, army hat and combat trousers. Its layers of societal tension came from its battle-ready design, not least the jacket's camouflage pattern for concealment, and the trousers' functionality for fighting. He stood and went over to a tree, used it as a toilet.

The benches lined a path, facing inwards. I sat down. Along the way, on the other side, someone young was sitting in a mustard vest. Their head was shaved, their clothing was beyond gender. They were there for a while. Eventually they stood and walked away. They had a black top tied round their waist, the bottom of it visible from the back. On it was printed 'UTOPIAS ARE NECESSITIES'.

I came to Gordon Square. No. 46, the house where the Stephen sisters first moved in 1904, is still standing; the place where they found autonomy and refused fashion. No longer a home, it's now offices for the nearby University College London.

In the centre, as with the other squares, was a public garden. A man exited. He looked pulled together in a pale chore jacket, buttoned up, with khaki utility pants that went tighter at the ankle. His outfit had the pleasing creative tension of individual pieces that each had energy, assembled for a particular equilibrium. He wore a baseball cap back to front. As he walked away, I could read its slogan: 'GOOD TIMES'.

In the square, a young woman was talking on her phone, wearing earbuds. She sat on a bench, a knife-pleat leather skirt fanned out around her. She stood. There was a longer black underskirt layered beneath, a brown crepe tank above. In her hand was a black leather trench. She put it on the ground, lay down, on her front. She had on black patent boots. She was no longer talking, just scrolling her screen. Here was a tension of display and concealment: look at me, but also, leave me alone.

A young man walked past in a black long-sleeve T-shirt, printed with a map of the planet as if cut flat, like the whole world were here to see. Two young friends came into the park and worked out their optimal spot: sun or shade? They sat on the grass in front of me. One was in a black striped T-shirt, and black tailored trousers, belted high to hold an elegant line.

It made me think of Maynard Keynes, who had also lived at No. 46, and those photos of him with his hand in his high-waisted trouser pocket, pushing out his crotch. So much has changed. If Maynard Keynes were alive now, he could just go on Grindr.

This young man wore his high-waisted pants with delight. His pleasure in wearing his garments, the success of the tension between T-shirt and tailoring, was clear.

His friend was in an oversized blue chore jacket and a yellow mini camisole dress. It was silk, about the same length as the jacket, held by little straps, with black lace at the chest. On her feet were black boots. The tension of her outfit was fantastic. It was some freedom.

Now, when I look at clothes, I think first about tension. It allows me to remove myself from the fashion industry's cycles, and to get closer to a garment's wearer. Who are they? Why do they wear what they wear? How would they like their life to change?

It also lets me consider its makers. By this I mean not just its designer, but those who constructed the garment, those who spun its yarn and wove its cloth.

With this new philosophy, we can move fashion to a fresh realm, within which we can each play an active role. We may have hope of lifting ourselves out of our toxic relationships with clothing, which can be damaging to our mental health, and are causing irrevocable damage to the planet. We may be able to use our garments to express and experience love.

The lovelessness of fashion, its meanness: these qualities are easily parodied by popular culture because they ring so true. Spending this time with the Bloomsbury group has pushed my thinking about garments wide open. My love of clothing is stronger than before, and it has utterly changed. I can now see a path to understanding.

I am closing my laptop to go and sew by hand. I am making.

Postscript

A few months later, my father, Tony Porter, died unexpectedly. He was hospitalized with pneumonia, exacerbated by his pre-existing heart condition. He was an artist, a teacher, a maker.

I had planned to write an appendix to the chapter on Vanessa Bell. I was going to detail how to make a rag rug, like those we saw on p.68. Grief pulls words back. Right now, I could not write jolly step-by-step instructions. Anyway, it would have been a lie. I taught myself rag rug making through videos on YouTube. Why write it out again, pretending it was my own knowledge?

It is so simple. Get a large crochet hook. Cut cloth into wide strips. Knot them together. I used an old linen sheet. My first row, crocheted with YouTube videos watched on repeat.

Autumn and winter have passed. I have started tailoring. First, I cut and hand-sewed a jacket from blue waxed cotton. It is like the uniform of a scientist from the space station, on which the observations of this book took place.

Next was a version in denim. I didn't order enough indigo cloth, so the back is a lighter denim than the front.

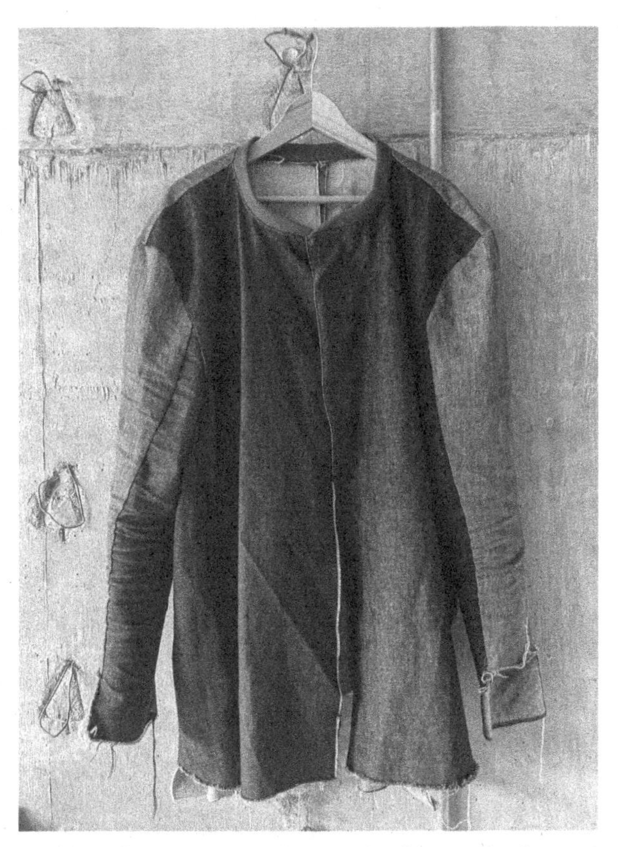

I have it on pretty much every day. I'm wearing it now, as I write these words.

After my mother's death, I grieved through making. In time, it became living through making. Since my father died, I am once again in the realm of making and grief.

A week after he died, I cut a pattern based on an old US prisoner's jacket, which I'd bought second-hand from Portobello Market in 1994. I hand-sewed it from deadstock slubby white wool cloth, added a rib collar. It's like the mechanic's uniform for the space station, though the cloth may be impractical for repairing a hyperdrive.

When I wrote of the change I had experienced writing this book, I was ready for it to be short-lived. It now feels life-long. I sew at dawn, on weekends, in evenings when I can. Grief can unshackle you, shift your identity, as the Stephen sisters found with their flight to Bloomsbury.

Making is now central to my lived philosophy. Here is the

finished rag rug, under the table where we work and eat. On the rug is our dog, Orpheus. Behind are the legs, foot and hand of my husband, Rich.

And then . . .

In February, I got a message from Francesco Risso, creative director of the Italian fashion label Marni. It was a few days before the brand's show, held during Milan fashion week, five months after this book was published.

Risso had read it. Virginia Woolf's words had activated him, causing him to entirely change his method of working. 'Pure instinct and "bring no clothes" was the fire that started it!' he wrote. 'Now it has become our mantra.'

I happened to be in Milan at the time. The next day, I went to see Risso at the Marni studio, as they made their final preparations for the show. He said that, previously, he would design collections using research and mood-boards. Reading the book had jolted him to try a new approach.

They covered the walls of the Marni design studio in paper, blocking out any images that may have been on the walls. Within this paper cave, he asked his design team to 'bring no clothes'. They created a collection without outside reference.

This is the result.

It was wild. Reviewing the show, *New York Times* critic Vanessa Friedman stated that Risso had 'boiled fashion down to its essence so it could begin again'. She wrote that Risso had 'birthed a very chic primal scream'.

Crucially, Risso had not created a Bloomsbury collection from 'bring no clothes'. Instead, the words had catapulted him someplace new.

At the end of *Tractatus Logico-Philosophicus*, Wittgenstein implores his reader to not dwell in his work. 'He must, so to speak, throw away the ladder after he has climbed up it.' This is what Risso did. This is what we must do.

Special Thanks and Acknowledgements

Bring No Clothes began from conversation with Nathaniel Hepburn, director of Charleston, and Susannah Stevenson, artistic director of Charleston Festival. They asked if I'd be interested in curating an exhibition on Bloomsbury and fashion. I said yes. I will be forever grateful to them for planting the seed, and letting it flourish.

It soon became clear that this could also be a book. I thank my editor, Chloe Currens, for her faith in the project, her guidance, wisdom, support, strength and friendship. Thea Tuck at Penguin has provided invaluable assistance throughout. Thank you to Matt Hutchinson, Sam Voulters and Danielle Pender, and to Sam Talbot and Isabel Davies. Rebecca Carter and PJ Mark are dream agents – thank you both.

I first saw mention of Woolf's words 'bring no clothes' in Alison Light's 2007 book *Mrs Woolf and the Servants*, to which I am indebted, not just for the quote, but also for showing the viability of alternative approaches to Bloomsbury. Works by other biographers and academics formed the bedrock, among them Hermione Lee, Frances Spalding, Wendy Moffat, Robert Skidelsky, Richard Davenport-Hines, Sandra Jobson Darroch, Miranda Seymour.

For years, Kim Jones has been helping to preserve the legacy of Bloomsbury. Without his work, this book would likely never have existed. Thanks to him, and to his team, especially Simon Parris and Lucy Beeden. Virginia Nicholson offered generous support to the project, as have Tobit Roche and Nancy Oakley. Maggie Humm has been a sounding board throughout, and I thank her. Gabriel Beard and Rita Keegan each separately gave me inspiration to start making clothes – thanks to them both, and to Alison O'Brien for her mentorship. I bought all the fabrics used in the book from the excellent Merchant & Mills.

Thanks to Olivia Laing and Ian Patterson for their encouragement and counsel; to Paul Flynn for the conversations around Victoria Park, and to Chantal Joffe for the space to think. Thanks to Hilton Als, Frances Armstrong Jones, Dan Beaumont, Laura and William Burlington, Morgan Clement, Chapter 10 Book Club and the Friends of Arnold Circus.

I send all my love to my sisters – Sarah, Sophie, Chloe – and to their families. Rich Porter is my love. He has held me through this time. I love you, Rich.

This book was built with the help of many archivists, librarians, curators and experts. Darren Clarke, head of collections and research at Charleston, provided early insight; Emily Hill, Miriam Phelan and Shannon Smith have been incredible comrades in research and development of ideas. Whenever I was at Charleston, I was happy to bump into the brilliant Kathy Crisp: she knows what is what.

Patricia McGuire, archivist at the King's College, Cambridge Archive Centre, has been the most valuable support throughout the process of writing this book. I would look forward to my visits to the Centre, and to what would be uncovered next. Thank you to Patricia, and to her colleague Tom Davies.

Rosemary Harden, manager of the Fashion Museum in Bath, was an early advocate for the project, and granted me access to the Ottoline Morrell collection. Collections manager Eleanor Summers guided me through the Morrell collection, shared knowledge and led me down the path of discovery.

The staff in the Manuscripts room of the British Library are excellent, as the staff are throughout the building, particularly the librarians in Humanities 1. I thank all who work at the British Library, particularly those whose labour there is unseen.

At the Tate Archive, archivist Darragh O'Donaghue helped me out many times: his work is greatly appreciated. David Thompson has been an immense help with images, as have the staff of its photography studio.

Many others have helped along the way: if I miss your name, apologies and thanks. At the Berg collection of the New York Public Library: Emma Davidson; at Bridgeman Images: Sian Philips; at the Charles Deering McCormick Library, Northwestern University: Kolter Campbell; at Coates Library, Trinity University: Colleen Hoelscher; at Guildhall Art Gallery, London: George Hunt; at Houghton Library, Harvard: James Capobianco and Zoe Hill; at The Keep, East Sussex: Tim Evenden, Rose Lock and Karen Watson; at McNay Art Museum: Dan Guerrero; at the National Portrait Gallery, London: Mark Lynch; at Scala Archives: Valentina Bandelloni; at Surrey History Centre: Julian Pooley; at Westminster Reference Library, London: Nick Osborne.

Quotation Reference Sources

Key:
BL – British Library
TGA – Tate Gallery Archive
KCC – King's College Cambridge
MHP – Monk's House Papers
CUL – Cambridge University Library
USL – University of Sussex Library
HRC - Harry Ransom Center
WC – Wellcome Collection

Introduction

P1 'We are hoping to see you . . .' Virginia Woolf, *The Letters of Virginia Woolf vol2,* p443 'My Violet, I will come on Saturday . . .' *The Letters of Virginia Woolf vol1,* p441 'Please bring no clothes.' *The Letters of Virginia Woolf vol1,* p478

P2 'don't trouble to dress . . .' TGA, 20078/1/44/1

P6 'I do not wonder that people commit suicide . . .' BL, MS 83202

P7 'Sapphist' *The Diary of Virginia Woolf vol3,* p51

P8 'As I told you brutally . . .' Virginia Woolf, *The letters of Virginia Woolf Vol 1,* p496

P12 'We must do away with . . .' Ludwig Wittgenstein, *Philosophical Investigations*, Part 1 Section 109 'the lovelessness that is so pervasive . . .'. bell hooks, *All About Love: New Visions,* pxxix

Virginia Woolf

P21 'in plain black dresses . . .'. William Rothenstein, *Men and Memories vol1*, p97 'like a cameo . . .' BL, ADD MS 88886/4/13

P23 'At any rate, the looking-glass shame . . .' Virginia Woolf, *Moments of Being,* p81

P24 'I was forced to wear certain underclothing . . .' Virginia Woolf, *A Passionate Apprentice: The Early Journals*, p64

P25 'I shrink from the years 1897-1904 . . .' Virginia Woolf, *Moments of Being*, p140

P26 'I read and wrote . . .' Virginia Woolf, *Moments of Being,* p151 'tidied and in our places . . .' Virginia Woolf, *Moments of Being,* p151 'At seven thirty we went upstairs . . .' Virginia Woolf, *Moments of Being,* p152

P27 'It was not velvet . . .' Virginia Woolf, *Moments of Being,* p153 'He at once fixed on me . . .' Virginia Woolf, *Moments of Being,* p153 'Have you any stays . . .' Virginia Woolf, *The letters of Virginia Woolf Vol 1*, P84 'it is astonishing what depths . . .' Virginia Woolf, *The letters of Virginia Woolf Vol 1*, P85

P30 'Everything was going to be new . . .' Virginia Woolf, *Moments of Being,* p201

'Vanessa and I were in a twitter of excitement . . .' Virginia Woolf, *Moments of Being*, p205 'criticised our arguments as severely . . .' Virginia Woolf, *Moments of Being*, p207 'What is good?' George Moore, *Principia Ethica*, p2

P31 'Vanessa, having said perhaps . . .' Virginia Woolf, *Moments of Being*, p206 'She knew how to read the people . . .' Virginia Woolf, *The Voyage Out*, p4

P32 'Each of the ladies . . .' Virginia Woolf, *The Voyage Out*, p9

P35 'Mrs V Woolf arrived after tea . . .' BL, ADD 83204

P36 'From all this, it is clear . . .' Virginia Woolf, *The Diary of Virginia Woolf, Volume One*, p34 'I am really in rags . . .' Virginia Woolf, *The Diary of Virginia Woolf, Volume One*, 1915-1919, p35

P39 'I am resigned to my station among the badly dressed . . .' *The Diary of Virginia Woolf vol1*, p284

P40 'no scaffolding; scarcely a brick to be seen . . .' *The Diary of Virginia Woolf vol2*, p13

P41 'the lovely gifted aristocratic Sackville-West . . .' *The Diary of Virginia Woolf vol2*, p216

P42 'She is utterly unaffected . . .' Vita Sackville-West, *Love Letters: Virginia Woolf and Vita Sackville-West*, p1 'She was smarter last night . . .' Vita Sackville-West, *Love Letters: Virginia Woolf and Vita Sackville-West*, p2

P44 'In this book, I have almost too many ideas . . .' *The Diary of Virginia Woolf vol2*, p248 'At once I feel refreshed . . ..' *The Diary of Virginia Woolf vol2*, p248 'To get to the bones . . ..' *The Diary of Virginia Woolf vol2*, p248 'Her evening dresses hung in the cupboard . . .' Virginia Woolf, *Mrs Dalloway*, p35

P45 'falling in love with women . . .' Virginia Woolf, *Mrs Dalloway*, p30 'ran along the passage naked . . .' Virginia Woolf, *Mrs Dalloway*, p32 'Now, where was her dress?' Virginia Woolf, *Mrs Dalloway*, p35 'How Shakespeare loathed humanity . . .' Virginia Woolf, *Mrs Dalloway*, p79

P46 'scissors rapping, girls laughing . . .' Virginia Woolf, *Mrs Dalloway*, p78 'And there were the shops . . ..' Virginia Woolf, *Mrs Dalloway*, p80 'human beings have neither kindness . . .' Virginia Woolf, *Mrs Dalloway*, p80 'for in all the hat shops and tailors' shops . . .' Virginia Woolf, *Mrs Dalloway*, p18 'claiming power over approximately 412 million humans, the vast majority people of colour.' http://theunbrokenwindow.com/Development/MADDISON%20The%20World%20Economy--A%20Millennial.pdf 'And her old uncle William used to say . . .' Virginia Woolf, *Mrs Dalloway*, p12

P48 'But my present reflection is that . . .' *The Diary of Virginia Woolf vol3*, p12/13

P49 'But I must remember to write about my *clothes* . . .' Virginia Woolf, *The Diary of Virginia Woolf vol3*, p21 'incredibly dowdy, no woman cared less . . .' Virginia Woolf, *The Diary of Virginia Woolf vol3*, p52

P50 'My own lack of beauty depresses me today..' Virginia Woolf, *The Diary of Virginia Woolf vol3*, p64 'Virginia looked supremely elegant in it . . .' *Recollections of Virginia Woolf by her Contemporaries* (ed Joan Russell Noble), p209

P52 'it was very forced & queer & humiliating . . .' Virginia Woolf, *The Diary of Virginia Woolf vol3*, p91

P53 'defend himself by attacking Todd's morals . . .' Caroline Seebohm, *The Man Who Was Vogue,* p127 'there is much to support the view . . .' Virginia Woolf, *Orlando: A Biography*, p170 'a biography beginning in the year 1500 . . .' *The Diary of Virginia Woolf vol3,* p161 'The change of clothes had . . .' Virginia Woolf, *Orlando: A Biography*, p170

P54 'If we compare the picture of Orlando . . .' Virginia Woolf, *Orlando: A Biography*, p171 'It was a change in Orlando herself . . .' Virginia Woolf, *Orlando: A Biography*, p171/172

P55 'I mean I think I am about to embody . . .' Virginia Woolf, *The Diary of Virginia Woolf vol 4,* p53 The Dreadnought Hoax

P58 'I suppose I must describe Monday's escapade . . .' BL, 58120A, 101

P59 'Five young men and one young woman . . .' BL, 58120A, 103

P60 'No one had the vaguest idea . . .' Quentin Bell, *Virginia Woolf*, p158

P62 'We went as pictures by Gauguin . . .' James Strachey, *Friends and Apostles, The correspondence of Rupert Brooke and James Strachey,* p164 'dress up as a South Sea Savage again . . .' Virginia Woolf, *The Letters of Virginia Woolf Vol1*, p455

P63 'dismayed at the whole idea' Quentin Bell, *Virginia Woolf*, p158 'will not show one ray of honesty . . .' Michèle Barrett, *Empire and Commerce in Africa, Woolf Studies Annual Vol 19* 'Two interviewers have been today . . .' *The Letters of Virginia Woolf Vol 1*, p422

Vanessa Bell

P67 'Had a bonfire & burnt Mrs Bells mattress . . .' BL, ADD 83219

P70 'When I got into the grubby, shabby, dirty world . . .' Vanessa Bell, *Sketches in Pen and Ink,* p73 'How did we ever get out of it?' *Selected Letters of Vanessa Bell*, p62

P71 'I remember that one well . . .' Vanessa Bell, *Sketches in Pen and Ink*, p75

P72 'not only with dresses . . .' Vanessa Bell, *Sketches in Pen and Ink*, p76

p74 'would come back & have late lunch . . .' TGA 8010.11.2

P75 described as 'eccentric' and 'formidable', https://www.exploringsurreyspast.org.uk/themes/people/artists/lushington/

p77 'The entertainment was frugal . . .' Vanessa Bell, *Sketches in Pen and Ink*, p100 'Of course the young men from Cambridge . . .' p101 Vanessa Bell, *Sketches in Pen and Ink*, p101 'always lived in my memory' . . .' Virginia Woolf, *Moments of Being* p212/213

P78 'He pointed his finger . . .' Virginia Woolf, *Moments of Being* p212/213 'It was, I think, a great advance . . .' Virginia Woolf, *Moments of Being* p212/213

P83 'It was to be a society of people . . .' Virginia Woolf, *Roger Fry,* p184 'How you have changed everything for me . . .' Vanessa Bell, *Selected Letters of Vanessa Bell*, p112

P86 'She and I are going to revolutionize our dress,' Vanessa Bell, *Selected Letters of Vanessa Bell*, p160

P87 'I should make or at least superintend . . .' Vanessa Bell, *Selected Letters of Vanessa Bell*, p174

P88 'I am going to make myself a new dress . . .' Vanessa Bell, *Selected Letters of Vanessa Bell*, p185 'My God! What clothes you are responsible for!' Virginia Woolf, *The Letters of Virginia Woolf vol 2*, p111

P93 'I came in from the garden . . ..' MHP, SxMs-18/1/D/62/2

P96 'I like clothes, if I can design them.' *The Diary of Virginia Woolf vol 2*, p146

Duncan Grant

P120 'As I was getting into bed . . .' Lytton Strachey, *The Shorter Strachey*, p12/13 'I was very happy . . .' Lytton Strachey, *The Shorter Strachey*, p12/13

P121 'Dearest Jambeau . . .' BL 60668, 91 'damn dress clothes'. BL, 60668, 122 'Dearest Duncan, Why aren't you a Cambridge undergraduate . . .' BL,57930A, 4 'I found in the end your coat . . .' BL, 57930A, 8 'I was very glad to get the photograph..' BL,57930A, 13

P122 'Dearest Duncan, Oh, I've got a third vision . . .' BL, 57930A, 35 'Dearest Maynard . . .' BL 58120A, 4

P123 'It was luckily a lovely day . . .' BL, 58120A, 109 'You may show any of the back views . . .' BL, 58120A, 119

P124 'Will you dine with us . . .' TGA, 20078/1/44/1

P126 'There was a most unpleasant story . . .' *Friends and Apostles, The correspondence of Rupert Brooke and James Strachey*, p153

P128 '3 handkerchiefs, 2 thick drawers . . .' KCC, RCB/M/12

P129 'Duncan passed through – a strange shaggy interlude . . .' *The Diary of Virginia Woolf vol1*, p240

P130 'after which Nellie . . .' BL, ADD MS 83202

P131 'After dinner Nellie & I . . .' BL, ADD MS 83202 p15

P132 'Duncan Grant the artist thinking to frighten us . . .' BL, ADD MS 83204, p9 The Apostles, and conversations about style

P144 'the whole individual . . .' KCC, GBR/0272/REF/1/10 'Is the soul more than raiment . . .' KCC, GBR/0272/REF/1/10 'And herein lies if we look for it . . .' KCC, GBR/0272/REF/1/10 'but that which society imposes on the individual members . . .' KCC, GBR/0272/REF/1/10 'Hear I pray thee the prayer . . .' KCC, GBR/0272/REF/1/10 'any particular convention that we object to . . .' KCC, GBR/0272/REF/1/10

P145 'Thus in this one pregnant subject of CLOTHES . . .' Thomas Carlyle, *Sartor Resartus*, https://www.gutenberg.org/files/1051/1051-h/1051-h.htm 'I think it is safe to say that there is a certain element . . .' USL, SxMs-13/2/O/2/A

E.M. Forster

P152 'I have a suit of clothes . . .' E. M. Forster, *Abinger Harvest*, p37

P153 'In a steamer with Sheppard from Kew . . .' E. M. Forster, *The Journals and Diaries of E. M. Forster vol1*, p143 'Reasons against suicide . . .' E. M. Forster, *The Journals and Diaries of E. M. Forster vol1*, p144 '. . .there's no doubt that . . .' E. M. Forster, *The Journals and Diaries of E. M. Forster vol1*, p157

P156 'one of the very last children . . .' p19 P.N. Furbank, *E.M. Forster: A Life vol1* p19 'I knew this was "wrong" . . .' E. M. Forster, *The Creator as Critic*, p212

P162 'It posits "a continuum between homosocial and homosexual . . ."' Eve Kosofsky Sedgwick, *Between Men*, p1

P166 'indescribably repellent' E.M. Forster, *Collected Short Stories*, p9 'attired in a dress coat . . .' E. M. Forster, Collected Short Stories, p27 'was a tall, weakly built young man . . .' E. M. Forster, Where Angels Fear To Tread, p51

P167 'And all the time, three little bundles . . .' E. M. Forster, *A Room with a View*, p150 'Clothes flew in all directions.' E. M. Forster, *A Room with a View*, p150

P168 'You've stopped me . . .' E. M. Forster, *The Journals and Diaries of E. M. Forster vol2*, p3 'Miss Stephen said the paper . . .' E. M. Forster, *The Journals and Diaries of E. M. Forster vol2*, p17

P169 'Typical of my feebleness . . .' E. M. Forster, *The Journals and Diaries of E. M. Forster vol2*, p43/44 'The life of the flesh is best . . .' E. M. Forster, *The Journals and Diaries of E. M. Forster vol2*, p44

P171 'hundreds of young men are at play . . .' *Selected Letters of E. M. Forster Vol1*, p236/237

P175 'I met Morgan Forster on the platform . . .' *The Diary of Virginia Woolf vol1*, p291 'I am happiest when busy . . .' E. M. Forster, *The Journals and Diaries of E. M. Forster vol2*, p57 'Morgan came for a night . . .' *The Diary of Virginia Woolf Vol 2*, p33

P176 'into a world of whose richness and subtlety . . .' E. M. Forster, *Abinger Harvest*, p15

P177 'And it is this undeveloped heart . . .' E. M. Forster, *Abinger Harvest*, p15 'There can be no love without justice . . .' bell hooks, *All About Love: New Visions*, p19/20 'the national figure of England is Mr Bull . . .' E. M. Forster, *Abinger Harvest*, p13

P178 'The main point of these notes . . .' E. M. Forster, *Abinger Harvest*, p25

P179 'I have forbidden my imagination . . .' E. M. Forster, *The Journals and Diaries of E. M. Forster vol2*, p63

P181 'I can go anywhere in it . . .' E. M. Forster, *Abinger Harvest*, p37

P184 'healthy, virile . . .' https://api.parliament.uk/historic-hansard/lords/1934/nov/28/metropolitan-police-accommodation

p188 'pretended I should kill myself . . .' E. M. Forster, *The Journals and Diaries of E. M. Forster vol2*, p85 'I have been happy for two years . . .' E. M. Forster, *Commonplace Book*, p94

P189 'I hate the idea of causes . . .' E. M. Forster, *What I Believe*, p18 'Naked I came into the world . . .' E. M. Forster, *What I Believe*, p25

P190 'The flat is Bloomsbury and insanitary . . .' E. M. Forster, *The Journals and Diaries of E.M. Forster vol3*, p48

P194 'Adding when I am nearly 85 how annoyed . . .' E. M. Forster, *The Creator as Critic*, p216

P195 'is due to the money behind it . . .' E. M. Forster, *What I Believe*, p21

Two Strachey and Carrington, or, The veil of clothing

P198 'What scandals! What disclosures!' Lytton Strachey, *The Letters of Lytton Strachey*, p54

P203 'You must know one could not do . . .' Carrington, *Letters and Extracts from her Diaries*, p17

P204 'You know I have always hated being a woman . . .' Carrington, *Letters and Extracts from her Diaries*, p324

John Maynard Keynes

P209 'They say that the boy . . .' CUL, GBR/0012/MS Add.7833 'ugliness . . .' CUL, GBR/0012/MS Add.7833 'I have a clever head, a weak character . . .' KCC PP/45/149/9 'My dear, I have always suffered . . .' KCC PP/45/316/155

P210 'Appearance is in fact relative . . .' KCC, UA/23/2/18

P212 'you could think and love what you liked . . .' Robert Skidelsky, *John Maynard Keynes: vol 1, Hopes Betrayed*, p77

P214 'and the talk which preceded it and followed it, dominated . . .' John Maynard Keynes, *The Essential Keynes*, p13 'The appropriate subjects of passionate contemplation . . .' John Maynard Keynes, *The Essential Keynes*, p14

P215 'I am no letter writer.' BL, Add MS 74230 'I feel that I want you very much . . .' BL, 57930A 'This is no letter at all . . .' BL, 57930A

P216 'Dearest Duncan, I am getting in the most miserable . . .' BL, 57930A 'I have taken the greatest care here . . .' BL, 57930A

P217 'general attitude . . .' BL, 57930A

P218 'I play badly but am much consoled . . .' BL, 57930A 'I think I shall have to give up teaching females . . .' BL, 57930A

P221 'becoming more fashionable than formerly . . .' BL, 57930B

P222 'in evening dress and very good looks' BL, 57930B 'the iron copulating-machine'. *Friends and Apostles: The correspondence of Rupert Brooke and James Strachey*, p55 'I hope you will find the enclosed useful' BL, Add MS 60672

P225 'hard, intellectual, insincere . . .' Lady Ottoline Morrell, *Memoirs 1915-1918*, p56

P226 'I work for a government I despise . . .' BL, 57931, 119

P229 'Dear Prime Minister, I ought to let you know that on Saturday I am slipping away from the scene of nightmare. I can do no more good here.' Robert Skidelsky, *John Maynard Keynes: Hopes Betrayed*, p374

P231 'nations are not authorized . . .' John Maynard Keynes, *The Economic Consequences of Peace*, p225 'The figure and bearing of Clemenceau ..' John Maynard Keynes, The Economic Consequences of Peace, p26 'carried no papers and no portfolio . . .' John Maynard Keynes, The Economic Consequences of Peace, p27

P232 'all sound and fury signifying nothing . . .' John Maynard Keynes, The Economic Consequences of Peace, p28

P234 'I sat in Gordon Square yesterday . . .' *The Diary of Virginia Woolf Vol2*, p120/121

P235 'poor'. BL,MS 57931, 133 'She's a rotten dancer . . .' Robert Skidelsky, *John Maynard Keynes: Hopes Betrayed*, p352

P237 'Forward rather than back . . .' E. M. Forster, *The Journals and Diaries of E. M. Forster vol 2, p47*

P238 'Keynes was no socialist . . .' John Maynard Keynes, *General Theory of Employment, Interest and Money (2007 Palgrave edition)*, pxxvi

P239 'enabled the Old World to stake out . . .' John Maynard Keynes, *The Economic Consequences of Peace*, p22/23 'Lancashire has found . . .' KCC, GBR/0272/JMK/C/2/1

P245 'Almost any measures seem to me . . .' KCC, SS/1/1-37 'I believe that for the future . . .' KCC, PS/3/114

P248 'THE AIMS AND OBJECTS OF THE EUGENICS SOCIETY . . .' WC, SA/EUG/A.30. p3 'In certain circumstances . . .' WC, SA/EUG/A.30, p4

P248 'In view of the possible effects . . .' WC, SA/EUG/A.30, p4 'to investigate the literature of race mixture . . .' WC, SA/EUG/A.30, p9

P249 'For my own part . . .' p374, John Maynard Keynes, *General Theory of Employment, Interest and Money,* p374

p250 'you could think and love what you liked . . .' Robert Skidelsky, *John Maynard Keynes: vol 1, Hopes Betrayed,* p77 'I remain, and always will remain . . .' John Maynard Keynes, *The Essential Keynes*, p22

P251 'genius . . .' https://www.ncbi.nlm.nih.gov/pmc/articles/PMC2986310/pdf/eugenrev00247-0048.pdf 'a terrible racist'. https://www.theguardian.com/world/2019/jul/13/ucl-inquiry-row-historical-racism-science-pioneers-rename-college-buildings What the Bloomsbury servants wore

P253 'My name in full . . .' BL, ADD MS 83202, p33/p39

P254 'boredom is increasing not decreasing.' BL, ADD MS 83202, p42 *'I do not wonder that people commit suicide . . .'* BL, ADD MS 83202, p42/43 Lady Ottoline Morrell

P269 'the top part of the face . . .' BL, Add MS 88886/4/12

P270 'stupid . . .' BL, Add MS 88886/4/9 'Spinoza I read a little every morning . . .' BL, Add MS 88886/4/8

P271 'You need never have one instants doubt . . .' HRC, Box 19 folder 1 'Rise up – rise up . . .' BL, Add MS 8886/4/4

P272 'so full of poignant memories and awakenings . . .' BL, ADD 88886/4/8

P274 'We became great, and intimate, friends,' Lady Ottoline Morrell, *The Early Memoirs*, p99 'It made my cape extraordinarily heavy . . .' Lady Ottoline Morrell, *The Early Memoirs,* p100 'I drank then of the elixir of Italy . . .' Lady Ottoline Morrell, *The Early Memoirs,* p101

P275 'I find it harder and harder . . .' Richard Ellman, *Oscar Wilde,* p43-44

P277 'It was odd the day of my marriage . . .' BL, ADD MS 88886/4/9

P278 'Do not live in the past . . .' BL, ADD MS 88886/4/4 'Elizabethan' Sandra Jobson Darroch, *Garsington Revisited* p5

P279 'there is no evidence that Ottoline had any Lesbian inclinations.' Sandra Jobson Darroch, *Garsington Revisited*, p194 'Lesbianism played no part in Ottoline's life'. Miranda Seymour, *Ottoline Morrell: Life on a Grand Scale*, p287/8 'The presence of a Friend. E.S.' BL, ADD MS 88886/4/4

P280 'I should love to have dinner (alone?) . . .' HRC, OMC, Box 29.6 'If only it may increase . . .' BL, ADD MS 88886/4/4

P282 'This summer I gave up work to art . . .' BL, ADD MS 88886/4/4 'One essential is not to spend . . .' BL, ADD MS 88886/4/4

P283 'Oh if you like it do it . . .' BL, ADD MS 88886/4/5

P284 'both so depressed at the military frenzy . . .' BL, Add MS 88886/4/5

P285 'know each other better co-operate . . .' BL, ADD MS 88886/4/5 'and Miss Virginia Stephen came to meet him . . .' BL, ADD MS 88886/4/5 'It is so delicious running on the grass . . .' may 22 1909

p286 'Philip would make me dress very smart . . .' BL, ADD MS 88888/4/6 'to see Paris Models . . .' BL, ADD MS 88888/4/6

P287 "All the horrid hard smart ladies . . .' BL, ADD MS 88888/4/6

P288 'superb in a magnificent gown . . .' BL, 58120A, 124/125

P289 'Men say, it is always in women's eye . . .' BL, ADD MS 88886/4/8

P290 'I feel nothing is more awful . . .' BL, ADD MS 88886/4/8

P291 'I had it so strongly yesterday . . .' BL, ADD MS 88886/4/8 'saying his love for me . . .' BL, ADD MS 88886/4/9 'One's character is like a casket of jewels . . .' BL, ADD MS 88886/4/9 'the last public word for Peace . . .' BL, ADD MS 88886/4/9 'Is it patriotic to ruin . . .' BL, ADD MS 88886/4/9 'Ottoline herself at the head . . .' *The Selected Letters of Vanessa Bell,* p175

P292 'Ottoline has a dressmaker . . .' *The Selected Letters of Vanessa Bell,* p174

P293 'you know I am a rebel . . .' BL, ADD MS 88886/4/9 'How mad England is to treat Ireland as they do . . .' BL, ADD MS 88886/4/9 'I shall always see in Asquith . . .' BL, ADD MS 88886/4/9 'I hate Asquith . . .' BL, ADD MS 88886/4/9 'Conscience Cottage . . .' BL, ADD MS 88886/4/11 'I love her very much . . .' BL, ADD MS 88886/4/9

P296 'Sometimes I think poor Brett . . .' BL, ADD MS 88886/4/11

P297 'Grow steel within you . . .' BL, ADD MS 88886/4/10 'The bird in my breast . . .' BL, ADD MS 88886/4/10

P298 'You know how much I have enjoyed myself . . .' TGA, 797/2/28

P300 'Poor dear, what an affliction . . .' TGA, 8010.5.692 'Is Ottoline becoming my rival . . .' *The Selected Letters of Vanessa Bell,* p85

P301 'Ottoline is slowly growing . . .' *Letters of Virginia Woolf vol 1,* p394 'I thought Virginia wonderful . . .' BL, ADD MS 88886/4/6 'It was a great surprise . . .' *The Letters of Virginia Woolf vol2,* p151 'My images, after leaving you . . .' *The Letters of Virginia Woolf Vol2,* p154 'Please don't treat me like an invalid – save for breakfast in bed (which is now a luxury and not a necessity) I do exactly as others do . . .' *The Letters of Virginia Woolf Vol2,* p158

P303 'you don't realise . . .' *The Letters of Virginia Woolf Vol2,* p188 'The walk in the rain . . .' *The Letters of Virginia Woolf Vol2,* p190 'A delightful letter . . .' BL, ADD

MS 88886/4/11 'She is exquisitely lovely . . .' BL, ADD MS 88886/4/11

P306 'poor old ninny . . .' *The Diary of Virginia Woolf vol1*, p175 'a ship with its sails rat-eaten . . .' *Virginia Woolf & the Raverats: A Different Sort of Friendship*, p93 Bloomsbury, fashion, philosophy

P318 'everything that can be thought . . .' Ludwig Wittgenstein, *Tractatus Logico-Philosophicus*, p30

P319 'how hard I find it . . .' Ludwig Wittgenstein, *Culture and Value*, p39e

P320 'Still I cannot get at what I mean . . .' *The Diary of Virginia Woolf vol 3*, p13 'The fact is that all archetypal images . . .' CG Jung, *Archetypes of the Collective Unconscious*, p13

P321 'And so our state and yours will be really awake . . .' Plato, *Republic*, 520 d

P327 'four-piece suit', Clive Bell Old Friends, p 120

List of Photographic Credits

Every effort has been made to contact all copyright holders. The publishers will be pleased to amend in future editions any errors or omissions brought to their attention.

Author's own photographs: 90, 91, 98, 100, 101, 105, 118, 138 161, 220, 266, 267, 276, 268, 305, 306, 309, 310, 311, 312, 313, 319, 325, 335, 336, 337, 338, 339. © Tate: 24, 33, 79, 85 (bottom), 94, 96, 119, 125, 126, 127, 128, 130, 131, 133, 134, 135 (bottom), 197, 203, 224, 230, 235. © British Library Board. All Rights Reserved / Bridgeman Images: 15, 95, 122, 223, 254, 256, 257, 258, 307. © The Henry W. and Albert A. Berg Collection of English and American Literature, The New York Public Library: 259, 35, 36. Reproduced by courtesy of The Charleston Trust: 8, 25, 28, 68, 69, 70, 75, 103, 104, 106, 107, 110, 229, 241 (bottom). MS Thr 564, Houghton Library, Harvard University: 23, 34, 38, 42, 47, 48, 54, 57, 72, 73, 81, 82, 83, 132, 142, 169, 176, 198, 260. © National Portrait Gallery, London: 22, 39, 51, 52, 58, 93, 146, 174, 199, 270, 273, 277, 278, 281, 283, 284, 285, 288, 290, 292, 294, 295, 302, 304. Harriott A. Fox Endowment, Art Institute Chicago: 16. Reproduced with permission of King's College Cambridge: 43 KCA JMK/PP/94/217, 135 (top) KCA FCP/7/3/1/68, 141 KCA KCAS/39/4/1, 155 KCA EMF/27/16, 156 KCA EMF/27/154, 157 KCA EMF/27/40, 158 KCA EMF/27/48, 164 KCA EMF/27/225, 165 (top) KCA EMF/27/249, 165 (bottom) KCA EMF/27/252, 168 KCA EMF/27/305, 170 KCA EMF/27/319, 171 KCA EMF/27/324, 172. KCA EMF/27/322, 173 (top) KCA EMF/27/322, 173 (bottom): KCA EMF/27/325, 178 KCA EMF/27/332, 179 KCA EMF/27/333, 180 KCA EMF/27/594, 183 KCA EMF/27/441, 185 KCA EMF/27/553, 186 (top) KCA EMF/27/445, 186 (bottom) KCA EMF/27/446, 187 KCA EMF/27/473, 191 (top) KCA EMF/27/629, 191 (bottom) KCA EMF/27/634, 192 KCA EMF/27/636, 199 KCA FCP/7/3/1/114, 200 (top) KCA FCP/7/3/1/219, 200 (bottom) KCA FCP/7/5/1/18, 201 KCA FCP/7/3/1/220, 202 KCA FCP/7/4/1/455, 204 KCA FCP/7/4/1/206, 205 KCA CP/7/3/1/213, 210 KCA JMK/PP/94/3, 211 (top) KCA JMK/PP/94/5, 211 (bottom) KCA JMK/PP/94/18, 213 KCA JMK/PP/20A/2, 214 KCA JMK/PP/94/29, 193 (top) KCA EMF/27/624, 193 (bottom) KCA EMF/27/639, 219 KCA JMK/PP/94/90, 222 KCA JMK/PP/20A/1, 225 KCA JMK/PP/94/159, 228 King's KCA JMK/PP/94/162, 233 KCA JMK/PP/94/165, 236 KCA JMK/PP/94/195, 237 KCA JMK/PP/94/174, 241 (top) KCA JMK/PP/94/223, 242 (top) KCA JMK/PP/94/282, 242 (bottom) KCA JMK/PP/94/284, 243 (top) KCA JMK/PP/94/300, 243 (bottom) KCA JMK/PP/94/331, 244 KCA JMK/PP/94/334, 246 KCA JMK/PP/94/387, 247 (top) KCA JMK/PP/94/397, 247 (bottom) KCA JMK/PP/94/435, 249 KCA JMK/PP/94/463, 251, KCA JMK/PP/94/479, 297 KCA FCP/7/4/1/44, 298, KCA FCP/7/4/1/44. © Estate of Duncan Grant. All rights reserved, DACS 2023: 92, 124, 181, 217, 226. ©Estate of Vanessa Bell. All rights reserved, DACS 2023: 80, 85 (top), 86 (bottom), 108, 154, 255. KCA © Paul Cadmus. All rights reserved, DACS 2023: 188. KCA EMF/27/1047 © Paul Cadmus. All rights reserved, DACS 2023: 190. © Victoria and Albert Museum, London: 29. © Fondation Foujita / ADAGP, Paris and DACS, London 2023: 50. A 1949 photograph of the statue of Sir William Mackinnon, originally erected in

Mombasa Kenya. Unknown photographer. Reproduced under a Creative Commons Attribution-Share Alike 4.0 International license: 61. Reproduced by permission of Surrey History Centre: 74. © Estate of Vanessa Bell. All rights reserved, DACS 2023./Victoria and Albert Museum, London: 84. © Estate of Duncan Grant. © The Samuel Courtauld Trust, The Courtauld Gallery, London / Bridgeman Images: 86 (top). Reproduced by courtesy of the Intellectual Property Office, https://www.gov.uk/government/organisations/intellectual-property-office, OWLS000347-1: 87. Reproduced with permission from the Charleston Trust © The Estate of Angelica Garnett and The Charleston Trust: 109. London, 1951, © Andrnea Frank Foundation: 143 (top). With thanks to Rachel Cole for permission to reprint the first page of Roger Fry's essay 'Shall we wear Top Hats': 143 (bottom). Courtesy of Bonhams: 152. Reproduced by courtesy of Steven Stokey-Daley: 160. Reproduced by courtesy of the Intellectual Property Office, https://www.gov.uk/government/organisations/intellectual-property-office, OWLS000343e. / KCA EMF/27/440: 182. Paul Cadmus, *What I Believe 1947-1948*, Tempera on panel. Collection of the McNay Art Museum, Gift of Robert L. Tobin /© Paul Cadmus. All rights reserved, DACS 2023, 194. © The Stapleton Collection / Bridgeman Images: 227. Private Collection © Estate of Augustus John. All rights reserved 2023/Bridgeman Images: 269. Reproduced courtesy of the Trinity University Coates Library: 275. Edith Helen Sichel aged 25 by unknown photographer, n.d. Public Domain: 280. © The Metropolitan Museum of Art/Art Resource/ Scala, Florence: 287. © Manchester Art Gallery / Bridgeman Images: 296. Lady Ottoline Morrell by Maurice Beck and

Helen MacGregor, reproduced by courtesy of the Intellectual Property Office, https://www.gov.uk/government/organisations/intellectual-property-office, OWLS000347-2: 308. © Comme des Garçons: 316. © Wiener Staatsoper / Michael Poehn: 317. Photographs by Giovanni Giannoni, courtesy (c) Marni Group SRL: 342, 343.